Hair Peace
BED Peace

PEACE AT LAST

the after-death experiences of
John Lennon

As Revealed Through

Jason Leen

Illumination Arts
Publishing Company, Inc.

Copyright © 1982 and 1989 by Jason Leen

All rights reserved. No part of this book may be reproduced or transmitted in any form without prior written consent of the Publisher, except for brief quotations used in reviews.

Manufactured in the United States of America.

Cover Art and Inside Illustrations by

>William Brooks
>Co-Creation
>P.O. Box 527
>Mossyrock, WA 98564

Library of Congress Cataloging in Publication Data

Lennon, John, 1940–1980 (Spirit)
    Peace at last: the after-death experiences of John Lennon/ as revealed to Jason Leen.
    p.   cm.
1. Spirit writings. I. Leen, Jason. II. Title
BF1311. L35L37   1989   133.9′3—dc20   89-2223
ISBN 0-935699-00-7: $11.95   CIP

Illumination Arts Publishing Company, Inc.
177 Telegraph Rd., Suite 361
Bellingham, Washington 98226

This book is dedicated to peace on Earth
and to the countless individuals who have
served this cause.

Acknowledgements

First I would like to thank John Lennon and the unseen host for allowing me to be the vehicle for this information. I would also like to thank my family for their loving support during the years I worked on the manuscript.

Very special thanks to Marisa Lovesong and John Thompson for their devotion to this project and for their ceaseless dedication to maintaining the quality of editing required for its completion.

Thanks also to William Brooks for his inspiration in creating the cover art and the interior illustrations — and to Don Grant for his guidance and insight on the cover concept and other artwork.

Finally, I offer my deep gratitude to all the personal friends who have given encouragement and support in various forms. Each of you in your own way helped make this book a reality.

Jason Leen

Many people have assisted in the creation of this book. To each of you we offer our deepest thanks. In particular, Eve Arno and Robert Hopper provided tireless and invaluable services during the final process of editing and arranging the text.

Special thanks also to Dr. Adrienne Brent for editorial assistance and encouragement — and to Carol Wright for cover design, layout, and other valuable guidance.

Among the many others who have provided love, support, and advice during the birth of this project are Diane Brandt, Vaughn Cox, Teresa Garrison, Joan Grant, Hank May, and Lori Porter.

The Publishers

Table of Contents

Introduction / ix

Author's Notes / xi

Editors' Notes / xvii

1 The Open Door: An End and a Beginning / 1
   John's Death / The Tunnel of Light / Julia Appears / Healed by Three Light Beings / Borderlands of Heaven / The Heavenly Decree / John's Message to Humanity / The Garden / Instant Travel / The Temple of the Octave / The Unlimited Nature of Humanity / The Chakras / The Second Temple

2 Peace At Last / 21
   The Third Temple / Discarding Illusions of Limitation / The Akashic Record / The Aura / Old Friends Appear / Divine Intervention in the Human Experience / Music—The Language of the Soul / "Judgement Day" / The Nature of Angels / The Keepers of the Gate / The Fourth Temple

3 The Journey of Awakening / 39
   The Keeper of the Flame / The Fifth Temple / The Great Hall / The Library / The Sanctuary of the Angels / Lady of the Living Waters / The Architects of the Human Body / Focus—To Prepare Earth / The Human Body / The Divine Nature of the Soul

4 Humanity: The Bridge Between Heaven and Earth / 55
   The Master Musician / Rhythm—The Universal Law of Divine Motion / The Primary Matrix / The Veil of Light / The Violet

Angels / The Sixth Temple / The Diamond Spiral / Julia Transcends / The Lightwave Embrace / The Seventh Temple

5 The Fountain of Light / 71
Humanity—The Primary Lifeform / The Primary Light Threshold / Earth's Journey Into A New Stellar Grouping / The Eight Geometric Forms Appear / The Transmission Begins / The Phase Shift Sequence / The Fountain of Light

6 The Body Electric / 83
The Human Cellular Structure / The Human Mind / Redesigning the Human Electrical System / The Formation of the Star Bridge / Redesigning the Central Nervous System / Five New Frequencies of Light / The DNA / Redesigning the Cells / The Final Phase of the Transmission

7 Ascension: The Destiny of Humanity / 105
Five New Frequencies Anchored Into Node Points / The Electrical Codes Are Released / The Entity of Earth / The Solar Being / The Solar Center of the Human Heart / Altering the Atomic Structure of the Blood / Light Codes and the DNA / The Divine Plan of Earth's Transformation

8 Heaven: The Kingdom Eternal / 119
The Stellar Being / Transition Codes / The Dimensional Shift / The Galactic Being / Earth's Destiny / The Dimensional Threshold / The Fountain of Light / The Lord of Creation

The Interview / 133

Glossary / 143

Introduction

IN LIFE JOHN LENNON WAS KNOWN FOR HIS EXPANDED POINT of view, repeatedly stepping outside the structure of accepted reality to swim in the ocean of possibilities. He now invites you to do the same.

Peace at Last is an account of Lennon's experiences on the other side of the door we call death — a door that is simply a transition from one aspect of ongoing life to another.

The most important message of this book is that **the unlimited potential of mankind is soon to be realized.** Our opportunity as humans on Earth is unsurpassed within the whole of Creation, and **there is no more exciting place to be than right here, right now.**

The theme of *Peace At Last* is similar to the wisdom expressed by Earth's great religions. Each one hypothesizes an ongoing reality that continues after death. Each describes a greater sense of self beyond the boundaries of physical existence. And each encourages the development of love, peace, wisdom, and a personal relationship with God.

For some people, this book will seem "just too far out" — at first. Even though we, as editors, have extensive metaphysical backgrounds, we still had to stretch to absorb some of its information.

After his journey through the tunnel of light, John is met by his mother, Julia. She serves as his heavenly guide and teacher, introducing him to various angelic and etheric entities. She then takes him to the Great Hall of Creation and its Sanctuary of the Angels, where his transmission to Earth begins.

In the Sanctuary we meet a master musician who assisted John with his earthly music, helping tailor it to appeal to a worldwide audience. We are present as John remembers the time before he took human form, when he planned his life and the things he would accomplish. He then realizes that everything is working out according to plan.

Numerous beings, including the "architects" who originally assisted in designing the physical body, describe changes we will be experiencing: direct access to divine energy through the DNA in each individual cell; five new chakras and frequency bands within our energy bodies as well as Earth's "body"; alterations to our endocrine systems and central nervous systems; changes in the atomic structure and functions of the blood; the ability to see and communicate with other forms of life on Earth; and direct personal communication with distant stars and planets.

In later chapters, two violet angels serve as John's personal companions and teachers. He is purified by fire (the Sacred Flame), by water (the Crystal Fountain), and cleansed eight times in the Temple of the Octave — finally transcending all remaining physical limitations to merge with the Lord of Creation.

Now he returns to tell humanity that **our destiny is to transcend time and space** — to unify our individual consciousnesses with each other, with our planet, and with God.

Since most of this information was transmitted to Jason Leen in 1981 and 1982, you might ask why this book is just now being published. Was the world ready for it in 1982? Were people open enough to receive John's message then?

We believe the human race has evolved rapidly during recent years — and that people are now ready to cooperate in creating a world of peace, love and joy.

For us, the material has been experiential as well as informational — a time-release capsule that has triggered mental, emotional, and spiritual growth — and we are still expanding with it.

John is sharing this information because he feels it is a vital and valuable tool — both for individuals and for mankind as a whole.

Since everyone's perceptions are based on his or her personal belief system, only you can decide what is valid for you.

The Editors
March, 1989

Author's Notes

Although most people would agree that John Lennon was very talented — even gifted — many will still wonder about his ability to dissolve the traditional barriers imposed by death. But John was never one to let tradition interfere with his desire to experience a more intimate relationship with Life.

Inspired by his openness and sensitivity, a whole generation of young people followed his lead. Now he asks us to view death in a very different way than we may have before. Having passed through the "illusion of death," freeing himself from its limitations, John now seeks to share what he has learned.

You may ask, "How?"

From birth I have been *clairaudient* — a French word denoting the ability to hear sounds originating at a distance, or beyond the normal human range. For many years I suppressed this ability, believing it had little or no relevance to living and working here on Earth.

Then during the early 1970s, while traveling along the border between Nepal and Tibet, I became intrigued by what the Buddhist monks called "direct transmission." In this experience two individuals, one living and the other dead, are linked in mental rapport. The living person is able to retrieve a wide variety of information, often leading to the completion of projects left unfinished by the deceased. Unlike what is commonly called "possession," no attempt is made by the deceased to control the living — the entire process is one of mutual respect and cooperation.

After returning from the Far East, I began an intensive investigation in the areas of sound and communication. I examined the possible connection between my clairaudience and the state of "direct knowing" which the early Christians and Essenes called *gnosis*.

My first major breakthrough came early in the morning on January 6, 1973. I began hearing a highly-energized woman's voice — and then an etheric form materialized in the study of my home. It was Almitra, an Arabic priestess. She had come to bring me a story. Little did I know that I was about to embark on a project which would encompass more than six years.

Several years passed before I realized this was the completion of a trilogy begun in the 1920s by Kahlil Gibran, the revered Lebanese mystic. The first book in Gibran's series, *The Prophet*, is considered a literary masterpiece and is one of the most widely-read books in history.

Before Gibran passed away in 1931, he had stated with certainty that his work would be finished after his death.[1] My bond with Gibran resulted in *The Death of the Prophet*, a book first published in 1979, then revised and republished in 1988.

Receiving the Gibran material was much like taking dictation, except that the energy was so intense at times it almost overwhelmed my physical body. In the beginning, it took all my strength just to hold the pen, and I was able to stay in that energy for only a few minutes at a time. This is why the book took so long to complete — the first chapter alone took six months.

John Lennon's information came through a somewhat different process, one I call "open consciousness interface." This technique does not require any form of trance or seance, and the receiver is totally awake throughout the communication.

Simply put, I attune myself to the vibration of the person wishing to communicate, and together we form a bridge of intent. The information is transmitted across this bridge. Then I put it into words that convey as closely as possible the intended form, content, and emotional essence of the person who is communicating.

---

1. Gibran was almost finished with the second book, *The Garden of the Prophet*, when he died. This book was later finished by Barbara Young, using a process similar to mine.

During the six years I worked with Gibran, I was amazed at the massive amount of interdimensional information being received by other people. It seemed as though a window had opened in the ethers and many of us were responding to the inflow of new energy. Rosemary Brown began receiving musical compositions transmitted by renowned composers from the past. Jane Roberts wrote a series of books on the nature of reality, revealed to her by a multidimensional being known as Seth.[2] The material coming through these and other channels supplemented the voluminous Edgar Cayce readings from the 1930s and 1940s.

As the flow of interdimensional information proliferated, I wondered if the world was being prepared for some extraordinary event. Once I heard John Lennon's revelation, the answer was clear.

The Lennon Adventure Begins

My first direct encounter with John came three nights after his death. I was alone in my home when I heard a voice, so moving and full of love that I felt it must be an angelic presence. The room filled with this message:

"Blessings, beloved brother. We come to you in the name of the Most High to remind humanity of its divinity. We ask that you aid a brother of the human race who was taken abruptly from your world. He has much to communicate to your people."

I agreed to do whatever I could, without knowing who was to be assisted. Then the voice said, "Jason, know your brother John."

I saw John Lennon's face as clearly as if he'd been there in physical form. Even though he was still in a state of transition, we were able to share a touching exchange of energy.

John didn't say much on this first visit. He did tell me that his

---

2. While creating these books, Seth spoke or "channeled" directly through Ms. Roberts. However, she also wrote two books using a process similar to mine. These relate the after-death thoughts and reflections of the philosopher William James and the artist Paul Cezanne.

deepest pain came from the thought of being cut off from his family. He stressed that he planned to continue communicating with the Earth. The visit was over very quickly, and I told no one but my wife what had happened.

The next day, December 12, nothing extraordinary occurred, but I did feel a definite shift within my body. I sensed my vibratory rate was being heightened so I could maintain a clear rapport with Lennon's new state of existence.

John returned the following day to tell me he was still in the process of being healed — that our visits would be short during this initial period of adjustment and would increase in length as time went on.

That first week John expressed concern for those who were grieving over his death. He said his etheric form was being pulled strongly by the millions of people calling him back to Earth.

Although deeply touched by the silent worldwide commemoration of his death, he wanted his mourners to move quickly through that period.[3] He remembered all too well his own anguish following his mother's death.

Our visits grew longer as we became more relaxed with each other. John continued to tell me about the healing experiences that were bringing his pain to the surface for release. The love and devotion with which the angels and other divine beings ministered to him was a great lesson for me. He said each of us on Earth is cared for constantly in the same loving, attentive way. Seeing him more radiant with each visit, I was convinced.

On Christmas evening, 1980, John announced that he was totally healed and free to go on with whatever he chose. He also told me more about our work together, calling it "our great adventure."

At our first meeting, John had said there would be a four-week transition period before our work really started. The coincidence was remarkable. January 6, 1981 was the day we started in earnest;

---

3. Yoko Ono requested a ten-minute memorial silence on December 14th, 1980 at 2:00 PM EST. Groups gathered at sites around the world to commemorate John's passing and to affirm peace in his name.

and my work on *The Death of the Prophet* had begun eight years earlier, to the day.

In early November 1981, John asked me to organize a book from the material assembled during our months together. He said the title, *Peace at Last*, perfectly expresses the message of the book and conveys the serenity he has gained and wishes to share.

It was John's decision to begin the book with the events surrounding his death. There have been many widely-publicized accounts of near-death experiences during recent years. Nearly all of these reports include trips through a tunnel of light similar to the one John experienced. Most descriptions stop there, however. To my knowledge, none contains the full spectrum of experience and information related in *Peace at Last*.

During the time we spent together, John asked me many times: "Will they believe?"

From my perspective, this account of his death and after-death experiences is so clear that its reality is obvious.

Healed of his pain and filled with love for all humanity, John Lennon has truly been transformed. What he shares now is divine truth, received first-hand from his own experience, from angelic sources, and from various aspects of Divine Mind. And by sharing his transformation, he has given each of us a priceless gift.

Jason Leen
March, 1989

Editors' Notes

Some of the terms used in *Peace at Last* are unfamiliar to most people. Therefore, we recommend that you read the glossary before beginning the text.

John's challenge in describing his adventures was that many of them were simply indescribable in the languages of Earth. He often encountered sights, sounds, and colors that were very different from anything he had experienced here. As a result, he quickly ran out of new descriptive words and expressions.

Many of the "future" changes described in this text have already taken place, even though they may not yet be perceivable by our physical senses. Some are now in process and others are soon to be initiated.

When the terms "your race" or "the race" are used, they refer to the entire human race.

In this text, the following terms have been used as names for God: the Father, the Creator, Mother / Father God, Divine Mind, the Primary Source, the Divine Presence, the Divine Force, and the Divine Source.

In the last chapter, the Lord of Creation appears to John in a form that resembles Jesus. It is our understanding that God manifests to each person according to his/her individual belief system or expectations.

PEACE AT LAST

....

the after-death experiences of
John Lennon

"Life is the childhood of our immortality."

GOETHE

One
THE OPEN DOOR: AN END AND A BEGINNING

You know how sometimes you sense something's wrong, but choose to ignore it? That's how I felt that night as I stepped out of the limo and started walking toward the Dakota.[1]

For several days I'd been feeling an incredible sense of change. At first I thought it might be the whole thing of "starting over." The album *Double Fantasy* really was a new beginning for me in many ways.

For the first time since Sean was born, I had ventured out of the househusband scene. I was out in the "real world" again — laying down new tracks and giving interviews. It was exciting!

I loved being back in the studio with Yoko; it felt great waking up in the morning with new songs in me head. There wasn't anything we couldn't do... or so I thought.

That afternoon at lunch we were discussing the increase of violence in the City. I hated to see this happening — it could only reinforce the distrust that already existed.

---

1. Lennon's residence in New York City.

We had a fantastic session in the studio that evening; but the nagging sense of change was starting to get to me. My thoughts kept drifting back to Sean. I even insisted we go right home after the session ended, rather than out to eat with the others.

The cold damp air stung my face as I walked toward the Dakota; my only thought was wanting to be inside and warm with Yoko and Sean.

Then I heard a man's voice. "Mr. Lennon."

I had barely turned around when the first bullet exploded into my chest — a second, a third... and I *knew* what was happening.

The lights around me grew brighter. My mind screamed, "Yoko! They have to save Yoko!" Then I was overcome by the incredible pain in my chest and waves of intense heat and nausea.

My body staggered up the steps and into the building; it must have been pure physical reflex. Somewhere in my mind the litany began: "Inside and safe... inside and safe" ... over and over, until I collapsed on the floor.

Falling...

                falling...

                                  falling...

I seemed to fall for all eternity — and then I was still... but only for an instant. My spirit body was vibrating so intensely that it could no longer be contained; and like several times before in my life, I was up and out of my body — my *physical* body, that is.

As I hovered near the ceiling I could see a man lying on the floor in a pool of blood. It was me. Yoko was screaming for a doctor — I'd never seen her in such pain. I tried getting through to her, to comfort her somehow; but she had totally shut down, trying to deny the reality before her.

With what strength I had left I focused on one urgent, heartfelt plea to Jay Hastings,[2] who was kneeling over my body: "*Help Yoko!*"

There was an indescribable pull on my spirit body. God I wanted to stay there and help Yoko! But there was nothing I could do. The pull kept getting stronger....

Then the brilliance in the room stabilized, and I felt a deep sense of peace. As I felt the release of my physical body, I knew it was dead.

A powerful surge of light filled the room, and the world I had known disappeared. I was being swept through a "tunnel" as bright as the sun itself. I had read about a tunnel of light in people's near-death experiences, but it was hard to believe this was happening to me.

As my speed increased, the gunshot wounds seemed to crystallize, like nuggets of some hard substance caught inside a softer texture. I was surprised I could still feel them, even though I'd left my body far behind.

---

2. The doorman at the Dakota.

Waves of music swept through me — it was the most beautiful symphony I'd ever heard. What a trip! The music kept coming — faster and faster — until it peaked in a great crescendo. I was in ecstasy!

Suddenly everything stopped. I knew I was out of the tunnel, but all I could see was light.

I felt someone near me. Maybe it was an angel... or....

Then I heard my name. "John."

That voice shook my soul. It was my mother! Julia! I never thought I'd hear her voice again. "I'm so glad to see you!"

She took me in her arms. She hugged me. She kissed me. I was *filled* with joy! I looked deep into her eyes. It really *was* her... Julia!

She looked so happy, so peaceful. Her body was more solid than mine, and more radiant. Would mine change in time? Did such a thing as time still exist?

This was all so different from what I had imagined. But what a relief to discover that someone really does come to meet you when you die. How perfect that it should be my mother — I had missed her so much.

"Thanks for coming, Mum. I'm really glad you're here."

"Oh John, I have been with you every day for years — if only you could have known. I want to be the mother to you now that I couldn't be on Earth."[3]

---

3. John Lennon was born during an air raid on October 9, 1940. His father left the family when he was quite young. John's aunt Mimi and Uncle George gave him a loving home, while Julia made a new life for herself. She wasn't very active in his life until he was a teenager. Then she bought him his first guitar

My whole body shook with painful childhood memories. Mum had held me during the air raids when I was little, and I used to pray to God that if the bombs did get me, he would see me safe to Heaven holding tight to mummy's hand.

The gunshots... they had sounded like bombs. And here was Julia. Was this heaven?

My thoughts flew to Yoko and Sean. What would they do? I hadn't even said goodbye.

Then a cool wind came to caress and soothe me; it carried me all the way back to Earth.

I could see their faces. They looked normal at first, but their expressions changed as layers of anguish and grief fell over them. What would they do now? My body flooded with pain. God I loved them! We were really a family. Sean and I were so close — and Julian.... I began to lose control.

Mother put her hand on my shoulder, and I was back by her side. Her love — and something about the light around us — helped me feel stronger.

"John, your greatest work is yet to come. But first, all of your pain must be surrendered; you must be completely healed and totally at peace."

∞   ∞   ∞

---

and taught him some basic chords. Just when they were becoming really close, Julia was killed in a freak accident near Mimi's home. John later referred to her death as "the worst thing that ever happened to me."

The light grew brighter and three angelic beings appeared, radiating the most beautiful colors I'd ever seen.

The colors inside their bodies flowed from their hands and became a waterfall of color, bathing me with millions of tiny spheres. I was glowing with three separate layers of light.

Then the brightest layer expanded until all three became one, and my wounds instantly blended into the rest of my body. There was no trace of them. Wow! This was great! If we could only do this on Earth.

Mum laid her hand on me chest, as did one of the angelic "light beings." Together they projected the same thought: "Be at peace." A powerful vibration filled my body, and I felt a deep sense of release.

What an incredible experience! Julia laughed as she shared my joy. "Welcome home, John. Welcome home!"

A magnificent landscape revealed itself all around us. I saw trees, water, flowers, birds, and animals — just like on Earth — only much more beautiful. The sights, the sounds, the fragrances all blended. It was like everything was made of light. I could smell it, hear it, taste it, all at once! Light was everywhere.

Could Earth ever have been this beautiful? Was this Paradise?

"Mother, where are we?"

"We are at the borderlands of what people on Earth call Heaven," she said. "We'll stay here until you learn to control your mental and emotional creations."

∞   ∞   ∞

I couldn't imagine a more beautiful setting. But she said these were borderlands.... How could Heaven be better than this?

"What do you mean by 'borderlands' of Heaven?" I asked.

Drawing seven circles in the air, Julia explained. "At this level of Creation there are seven interwoven realms of existence and experience. Each one directly influences what happens in the physical worlds.

"When these realms are united, an eighth is formed. The completed eighth realm is called Heaven. The borderlands will not seem so enchanting once you have experienced the transcendence of Heaven. They are to be held in no less esteem, however. All worlds are heavenly, as all share the same Creator. Earth itself is a form of Heaven, though it is presently 'asleep.'

"The time is coming for the Earth to awaken, but first it is mankind who must awaken and arise."

"On Earth you can recognize seven degrees of awareness: atomic, mineral, vegetable, animal, human, etheric, and angelic. There are also seven colors in the rainbow: red, orange, yellow, green, blue, indigo, and violet.

"These colors relate directly to the seven energy centers in your etheric body, known as chakras. Each chakra center corresponds to one of the seven glandular centers of the endocrine system: the gonads, Lyden glands, solar plexus, thymus, thyroid, pineal, and pituitary.

"Throughout your life on Earth, your chakras received energy directly from the seven etheric realms. The chakras step down the vibratory rate of the energy and disperse it through the glandular centers. Without this nourishment, the body cannot maintain itself on Earth."

"So where are we right now, Mum? Which realm is this?"

"We are in the third etheric realm. It has many names, but 'The Garden' is most popular. Our Mother/Father God has selected the perfect setting for each phase of your growth. Here you will be prepared for the experiences that lie ahead.

"I have been counseled by some of the most advanced souls in the kingdom in preparation for your coming. We have much to do.

"The decree has been given: **'No longer shall mankind fear death!'** You are being asked to help the people of Earth understand that death is only an illusion. They must release their fear of death in order to know the truth of their own immortality. Only then can they fully embrace the joy of living and the blessing of Life.

"'Through one of their own who is taken before them shall they find their way.' That prophecy describes many men and women at different times in Earth's history. It pertains to you as well.

"In order to speed your mission you will skip the 'cleansing' and the 'choosing.' These processes are part of the purification and vibratory alignment following death. They are not painful, but can involve long periods of soul-searching. Many newly-arrived souls submerge themselves in denial during these periods — first refusing to believe they died, and then refusing to believe they still live.

"When souls first arrive, most just want to rest within the

Valley of the Final Sleep. They can take as long as they like to adjust to their new reality. Your transition has been accelerated, however, so that your work can begin as soon as possible."

"What's this work you keep referring to?" I asked.

"The fear of death has enslaved mankind for æons," she replied. "This illusion cannot be allowed to continue."

"And I'm going to tell them there's no such thing as death?" I asked.

"John, on Earth you were known as a spokesman for world peace. Many people loved you, and still love you. The way is being prepared. They will listen to you again."

My mind was whirling with a thousand questions. But somehow I knew I'd get my answers soon.

∞   ∞   ∞

Scanning the horizon, I asked, "So what is the Valley of the Final Sleep?"

"All through history, religious books have spoken of this valley," she replied. "In recent times it has been called the *Hall of Judgement* or *Day of Judgement*. It is a place for refreshment and completion, a pausing-point within the constant activity of Creation. Those who enter this valley sleep the *Sleep of the Ages*, and when they wake they never need sleep again. There is peace at last."

A deep emotional response welled up inside me.

"In this valley," she continued, "souls evaluate their life's experiences so those they judge to be 'mistakes' will not be projected into their futures. By the time they are ready to leave, all fears have dissolved and each heart is completely open to the Father. This is one of the most glorious moments in all Creation. The wandering one has returned home."

Suddenly a flock of iridescent birds filled the sky — they were all the colors of the rainbow. An endless stream of questions filled the sky of my mind, somehow mirroring the flight of the birds.

Again my thoughts flew to Yoko and my two sons. So many memories. Love seemed to determine which memories I recalled — people and places I had loved, times I had felt loved. My heart cried out to my family...

> I love you with a love that knows no reason.
> I love you with a love that knows no season.
> I love you!

With her arms around me, Mother whispered, "I know how you feel to have died so suddenly. Remember, that's the way I left *you*. There will be a way for you to make your feelings known, but first you must learn more about these realms.

"No matter where we are, John, our existence and experience is dependent upon a vast assortment of energies and vibratory alignments. Most people are not aware of this while on Earth. I never tried to understand such things when I was there; they would have seemed foolish and a waste of time.

"But in this realm, everyone understands. Here we know we create our realities through exchanges of energy.

"One of the greatest challenges of life on Earth is to fully accept our creative powers. We have glimpses of these abilities, but most people dismiss them, saying 'that's just a coincidence.' For example, remember how often you thought of someone, and within a short period of time they contacted you? And how often did you know who was on the phone the instant it rang? Think of all the times you 'just knew' something — and it was true.

"In the etheric realms, we use telepathy to communicate; just the thought of someone or something brings us into immediate contact. And your free will is so expanded here that truly 'as you believe, so shall it be.' Every desire is instantly fulfilled. This is why you must learn to govern your thoughts before you can enter into a full relationship with your new reality."

"All of Creation is a thought in the mind of God. Everything is a mental creation and God is the creative power that brings it into form. This is truly the Key to the Kingdom."

"Well then," I mused, "if every wish is granted here, and money can't buy success or power — equality is finally achieved."

"You've got it!" Julia laughed. I laughed too. This was great!

∞ ∞ ∞

"Your mind was so altered at death that you are now perceiving time and space in a whole new way," she said. "There are no spatial limitations here, so travel is instantaneous. Learning to travel is an important next step for you, and it's simple; so relax and let's begin.

"Close your eyes, then visualize yourself a few feet ahead of where you are. You may feel a slight vibration."

I did feel a bit dizzy at first, but when I opened my eyes I'd moved to the exact spot I had chosen.

"Great game, Mum!" I laughed and made a few little side trips. The dizziness went away as I got the feel of it.

"Thought knows no distance, no boundaries," she said. "You can go anywhere your vibratory rate will allow you to enter. See that hill over there? I'll meet you at the top."

I smiled, remembering games we had played when I was very small. I used to race me mum for short distances, feeling very big and strong when I won. Now we both closed our eyes and arrived on the hill at the same time.

Before us was a beautiful grassy glen, but I'd never seen grass like this before. Each blade sparkled like the finest emerald on Earth. Flowers of amazing colors and fragrances were everywhere — and they were making soothing *sounds*. I could hardly believe my ears!

Surrounding the glen were dazzling white and silver trees filled with the flock of iridescent birds I'd seen earlier. Crystalline ferns — standing nearly twenty feet high — were woven among the trees. They swayed gently, as if floating under water.

Suddenly everything was silent. I looked toward Mother, but she stood with her eyes closed. The flowers seemed to float above the grass, suspended in mid-air. The birds had stopped singing... and nothing moved. The stage seemed set for something — or someone.

One solitary musical tone filled the air. I couldn't say when or where it began... but as I listened, an enormous crystal lotus flower appeared in the glen.

An opening formed in its side. "The time has come, John. This is the Temple of the Octave. This is your beginning."

What did she mean by my "beginning?" I hesitated, but only for a moment.

With eyes closed, I moved with her to the entrance. As we stood in the golden light of the Temple, the single musical tone unraveled into a fascinating symphony of sound.

"You must pass through the Temple eight times," Mother said. "In reality there is only one Temple, but it has the ability to manifest within the entire frequency range of mankind's development. Each time it will manifest in a different valley, and each valley will be more beautiful than the last. Your body will be completely healed and cleansed — nothing will remain in your entire being except light, purified and radiant.

"Prepare yourself for an extraordinary experience!"

Inside the Temple was a being shining so brightly I had to look away. At the same time there was a gentleness and love I'd never felt before.

A tidal wave of energy surged through me, each particle containing the essence of Creation. Millions of earthly images were reflected in that wave.

The energy made me strong enough to look at the being

again — but any form that may have been there was now transparent in the light. A stream of energy flowed from the center of the light and merged with some sort of harplike instrument. The being blended its energy with the multicolored "light strings," creating a beautiful, healing music. It was amazing! This music was *alive*!

Images of Earth flowed faster and faster, fusing into one solid ray of white light. The energy kept getting higher — the whole Earth seemed to course through my body!

I began to understand what was happening. This being was transforming light from higher realms into the energy perceived on Earth as sound.

The "lightsound" flowed through me, seeking out all aspects of my new body that weren't in harmony. These earthly aspects were absorbed within the millions of different images and sounds of the wave, then gently taken from me. Like unto like, I thought. The Earth was claiming her own.

As my awareness grew, I noticed subpatterns in the wave of energy — like little ripples you see when wind ruffles an ocean wave. They moved around me in all directions, until I was completely surrounded by intricate patterns of light.

The light grew even brighter, pulsing and glowing until it formed a solid crystalline sphere.

My whole body resounded with the music of Creation. In the joy of the moment I felt a unity with all others who have "heard the angels sing."

The music stopped... and we were back in the glen, surrounded by the trees and flowers. The birds were singing again and everything looked like it did before the Temple appeared.

"Wow! Did all that really happen?"

"Yes, John. Your experience was very real. The light beings in these Temples are among God's most magnificent creations. But they are no greater than mankind.

"I know it's hard to understand from your present point of view, but stay with me on this. People think angels have a higher spiritual nature than humans, but they really don't. If humans would focus their own divinity as intently as angels do, they would outshine the entire angelic kingdom. The Biblical passage — 'God made man in his own image' — is very true. Man is the image of the Image Maker.

"These great beings in the Temples are impressive in their ability to focus the light. In this realm they are the source of their particular ray of light energy. But they are limited to using only the energy held within their individual frequency range.

"In contrast, **when humans become fully aware of their divinity, they will be able to use the *entire* spectrum of creative energies and will have unlimited access to *all* the realms of Creation.**"

∞   ∞   ∞

The vitality I absorbed in the Temple was growing inside me. "I feel fantastic, Mum! Are the other Temples really necessary now?"

"Slow down John; school's not over yet. Many levels of your being are still unknown to you.

"The seven interwoven realms of existence I told you about earlier are separated by frequency differences, rather than distances of space. They exist simultaneously and are made of the same substance; but each vibrates at a different frequency rate.

"Remember the Bible verse where Jesus said, 'In my Father's house are many mansions?' Each 'mansion' is a different realm, or kingdom, and each is complete within itself. One of the greatest blessings of Creation is that 'bridges' exist between the different realms, giving us access to all worlds."

A *real* Magical Mystery Tour, I thought.

"Within each bridge two realms are wed, creating a perfection and harmony greater than either contains within itself. These connections are known throughout the cosmos for the peace experienced there. Humanity refers to one such bridge as Heaven, but very few people on Earth have fully understood this.

"I spoke earlier of the seven realms, the seven degrees of awareness, and the seven chakra centers. The harmonic combination of the parts in each of these systems creates an eighth, which is the completion of the whole.

"So it is with your etheric form. The chakras correspond to neural circuitry encoded in the subatomic features of your mind. Each circuit is vibrationally sealed and protected, so each one must be cleansed and healed with a different frequency. Therefore, **the Temple of the Octave expresses in eight separate frequencies to facilitate the healing of each individual circuit.**"

That's just like the seven notes in an octave of music, I thought to myself. When you add the eighth note, you have a completion — then you can make melodic chords. This was starting to make sense.

Julia motioned to a hill on the other side of the glen. I closed my eyes and moved instantly to the top. What she told me was true — the valley below really was more beautiful than the last.

"There are several reasons why each valley will appear lovelier than the one before. Primarily, the valleys have increasingly-higher vibratory rates. Your etheric senses are much more sensitive than your physical senses were, so they are able to perceive finer aspects of visual beauty after each cleansing in the Temple. Your entire nature is altered and you can understand concepts you may have avoided while on Earth."

I could buy that. I could think of at least a dozen concepts I avoided until I met Yoko. Even then there were some areas I just couldn't get into, though I read a lot and pursued me curiosities down some pretty unlikely avenues.

∞   ∞   ∞

The Temple appeared in the second valley, but this time its color was slightly different. Again, a single musical tone rang out — I could feel it through my whole body!

We closed our eyes and moved to the entrance. Again we were bathed in golden light before we went in.

The music of this Temple filled me with an overwhelming sense of compassion. My only desire was to radiate pure love throughout eternity.

Waves of intense energy poured through me, and at first I

couldn't tolerate the light of the being in the Temple. When I could focus again, I saw a whirling swarm of diamond "fireflies" creating an energy vortex that penetrated the center of the light.

A series of diamond-etched patterns streamed from the vortex, surrounding my etheric form and creating a song that filled me with every emotion I'd ever experienced.

Then, one by one, my emotions were gathered and absorbed by this energy — leaving me with a feeling of purity and innocence I had only imagined before.

∞   ∞   ∞

"It can be revealed to one person in a moment, what has been denied to all of humanity for æons."

KAHLIL GIBRAN

Two
PEACE AT LAST

THE THIRD VALLEY WAS A WORLD OF CONSTANTLY-changing forms, colors and sounds — and I could *feel* everything with every part of my body! Mum was obviously enjoying my enthusiasm.

"Why is this valley so unstable?" I asked.

"The first two valleys are still connected with the physical worlds," she replied. "This third valley is a transition point where physical matter is beginning its change back into etheric substance. Stabilization into any one form cannot occur, since there are no complete affinities between the physical and etheric realms.

"Here you will release the last illusions of limitation you accepted when you took on Earth's *veil of forgetfulness,* and you will begin to know your true nature."

My mind shifted to the Temple. What was going to happen this time? I wondered if it would be anything like the last.

Mum hugged me and kissed my cheek. "You must go in alone this time, John. Know that my love is with you all the way. I will be here when you return."

The Temple of the Octave materialized again... and the energy in the glen pulsed, as though some unseen source of power moved through the valley. Another tone resonated from the Temple.

We closed our eyes and instantly stood at the entrance. A shower of microscopic "diamonds" bathed me in light as I willed myself inside.

I was standing in a huge diamond — like a sun surrounded by countless mirrors. The radiance was so intense I could barely open my eyes. When I could focus, light was streaming through the crystal structure, creating a kaleidoscope of patterns and tones.

Somehow, I was beginning to understand where I was. In the third Temple, mental energies are condensed into physical form.

I felt more alive than ever! This diamond Temple seemed to be alive as well, its rhythms merging into a basic breath-beat. In... out. In... out.

The lights around me pulsed with a soft golden glow, and my own breathing slowed, forming a background beat for the music.

Every time I exhaled, the images in my mind were projected into the facets of the diamond. Each image took on its own reality. Yoko and Sean were everywhere. Images of Yoko merged with a heavenly blue ocean, while schools of fish filled the sky. Sean's face appeared in every cloud and his voice echoed in my mind. "Daddy, Daddy... "

My family was my greatest success. What were they going to do now?

A thousand answers were reflected on the facets around me. Some showed Yoko and Sean years in the future. But if only a little time had passed on Earth since my death, what were these images? Where did they come from? What did they mean? Which were true?

Mother's voice gave me the answer. "I can only reach you for a moment, John, to tell you that these are possible solutions to questions you asked on Earth. Since I wasn't there when they were formed, I won't attempt to translate them. But I can tell you this: even those that seem to be of the future were created by you in the past and stored as memories. Some may manifest, but most will not.

"Don't be concerned; they will be gone when you leave this Temple."

The music grew louder, flooding my mind with memories. Every song I'd ever written was woven into that music: words I had said, words I wished I had said, words I never intended to say, and words I should never have said at all.

Words. A lifetime of words... and much more. All of it flowed from my mind and was reflected in the crystal facets. Then they were absorbed into the diamond, each one forming an intricate multicolored design. It seemed they were somehow being collected and recorded.

Without these images, my mind broke through the mental barriers I had erected while on Earth. My body was ignited with a spectacular flash of lightning, and I expanded at an incredible rate of speed — encompassing universes in the blink of an eye. A million stars merged within my ever-expanding consciousness.

My life on Earth flashed before me, but I was no longer attached to any of it. As much as I felt I should be, and as hard as I tried, *I was simply not attached.*

I'd been too involved with my inner experiences to notice the being in the Temple. Now it revealed a barely-visible form. Its energy blended so perfectly with the facets in the Temple that it took a concentrated effort to make visual contact.

Flashes of dense golden light pulsed from the being. I felt loved — unconditionally loved — *because of* who I was and *in spite of* who I was.

My joy became a whirlwind, spinning me faster and faster, until I thought my body would fly apart — then I seemed to be standing still again! Internally there was a sense of incredible movement and an intense vibration, but on the surface I stood absolutely still!

I was now in direct contact with the being; and through the depth of our rapport, I began to understand what was happening. The atoms in my earthly body, and their many sub-atomic particles, had exact counterparts in the etheric realm. These etheric counterparts formed my new light body. But it was still connected to the Earth's vibration and needed to be released. That's what was happening now.

My whole being resonated with the energy surging through me. In the embrace of that light, my soul fused with Divine Love.

∞   ∞   ∞

"Life here will be much easier for you now." I was back in the glen, and Mother was there to meet me. But now I noticed a thin band of gold around her body. I looked at my hands and saw the same energy around me.

"This golden light has always been within your soul, John. It bonds you directly with God.

"When the physical body dies, the aura flares in a sensational display. At the moment of your death, I enveloped your aura with the golden light of my own soul. Your energies then stabilized and coalesced into your present form. The healing in the waterfall of color opened you to direct divine inspiration. Then, in order to manifest divine assistance, the Temples began to appear.

"It is important to know that not everyone experiences these events in the same way. Your relationship with each phase is unique — everyone's is. Even the sequence of the Temples is adjusted to align with the inner realities of each individual.

"But you have touched only the surface of these realities; the full depth of your being is still beyond your present comprehension.

"Now you can understand why I couldn't go with you into the third Temple. A different frequency is required to release each mind, so it is not possible for two people to share this experience.

"The intricacies of the human brain are perfectly mirrored in the facets of the diamond. As the being resonated, the images stored within your mind were projected onto the Temple's inner design."

That made sense. I couldn't imagine *not* going through this experience alone.

"The clearing of the mind takes place under many different circumstances. For most people it happens within the Valley of the Final Sleep. You bypassed that valley, so this way was designed to fit your needs. The perfection of our Father's care is infinite."

∞ ∞ ∞

The continuing sensation of internal movement was almost overwhelming.

I looked around the valley. Forms were constantly emerging from the rhythmic interplay of colors. Golden globes of light spun rapidly inside trees of vibrant green energy. The flowers were in a perpetual state of change, radiating their perfumes in delicate multicolored patterns. With my expanded vision, I could see thousands of hues in each color.

Little vortexes of musical energy danced around the valley, and a number of familiar faces flashed through my mind — faces of people who had died before I did. Most of them looked younger than I remembered, but each was easy to recognize. In a series of images, I was taken through my relationship with each one from beginning to end. I now knew my friends in ways I'd never even imagined. I was astonished! Then I wondered if they knew me as well as I knew them.

Julia's voice entered my thoughts. "Although you can't fully perceive them yet, a number of people who loved you are gathering to greet you. They are appearing to us in the form of these small energy vortexes.

"Your friends are vibrating in harmony with divine energy — expanding to realize their full potential. Unity with God is not just an idea here; it is a basic reality. Each soul is actively involved in expanding this awareness, and everyone feels joyously alive."

How different from my life on Earth. I remembered feeling so much guilt when I was there. It was really hard sometimes to be loving to myself or anyone else — and yet I knew I wanted to be; that's what most of me life was about.

Mother sensed my thoughts. "True peace starts with loving yourself. Perhaps by communicating that to the people of Earth, you will help them be more gentle and loving to themselves and to each other.

"As you gain more affinity with the etheric realms, you will be able to perceive and communicate with all who live here. However, you have deeper affinities with a certain group of individuals, and your primary interactions will be with them.

"The work you are being prepared for involves many elements of Creation and other groups of souls, as well as the Creator.

"**There is to be divine intervention in the human experience. People are starving in a land of plenty and desperately need to accept divine nourishment.** They have become too rigid, denying their spiritual inheritance. We must lovingly remind them of the infinite realms of Creation.

"Millions of people loved you, and still do. You have been chosen from among your co-workers because you have the greatest affinity with the human race. Still, the choice is yours. **The sacred gift of free will can never be revoked.**"

The opportunity to help humanity become a peaceful, loving family had been a lifelong dream. Could it be coming true?

∞   ∞   ∞

The small energy vortexes gathered around us and started to vibrate intensely. Again the faces flashed before me, filling my mind with bits and pieces of conversations I had shared with these people on Earth. Words and faces merged into a heavenly choir: "Welcome home John! We love you!"

A strange sensation moved through me, altering my form in some mysterious way. I was startled when a loud tone echoed through the valley. It was coming from inside of *me*! My joy at recognizing my friends — not lost, not dead, but very much alive — simply could not be contained. It had burst forth as *sound*!

"The music you created is the language of the soul," Julia said with gentle amusement. "Music is the natural vehicle for communication here. This reunion with old friends brought you great happiness, and so your response was one of joy.

"Many of them exist on other levels of the Kingdom. You will be even more delighted when you can know them in their current realities. At present, you could not tolerate the frequencies they radiate. Your own energy is being altered, however, so you can relate to *every* aspect of Creation.

"After you have experienced all eight phases of the Temple,

you will no longer be influenced by the limitations of the physical worlds. Then you will truly be free."

"Everyone here has unlimited access to knowledge of the physical worlds if we choose to use it," Mother said. "Many do not. They become so sensitive to vibratory emanations that they avoid interacting with energies as discordant as those on Earth at this time. Most of us rarely venture forth into those energies, even as mental images."

"Then how did my friends know I was here? Did they know when I died?"

"No, they didn't. I was the one who was asked to wait and watch, standing beside you even as you were being shot. There was no need for another to experience that. God strengthened me so I would have the courage to witness the pain that followed.

"I, too, learned much from that experience. I was able to seal your physical body almost instantly, and saw your etheric form emerge surrounded by a beautiful brilliance.

"Your friends knew you had arrived because of what happened in the last Temple. The images you released into the diamond were transformed into pure energy, which then radiated throughout these realms."

So — no secrets here, I mused.

I wondered about my experiences in the third Temple. "Were my memories being transformed as their images changed into the colored designs?"

"Partially," she replied. "The information was released as

the color codes formed. But more importantly, your entire earthly experience was recorded within the *Akashic Record*, also known as the *Mind of God* or *Book of Life*. Everything within the worlds of matter is eternally recorded there.

"In its primary stage, each atom of matter exists as spirit. When it leaves pure spirit to take on a denser form in the material worlds, its 'mission' is recorded in the Akashic Record. When it returns, all of its experiences are entered there.

"The difference between the two is revealed during what many people on Earth call *Judgement Day*. But it is not what most people imagine. The popular conceptions of Judgement Day have been created entirely through fear. This is not a judgement of God, followed by punishment or reward. *It is simply a time of recording.*"

"Thoughts, and the creative energies that form mental images, are highly magnetic in nature. Any thought generated in the etheric realms brings immediate results."

The same thing happens on Earth, only in slow motion, I thought to myself.

"Until the images of the mind are completely released, a soul cannot know lasting peace. When you released your mental images into the creative matrix of the third Temple, you also released the magnetic attraction between them and yourself.

"The fragments of our personalities which were in constant conflict on Earth become fused into one loving whole. We are literally reborn and swept into a completely new reality — one that demands our full attention. Therefore, we must release the old in order to receive the new.

"When you emerged from the third Temple, your memories no longer existed in your own mind, but they weren't destroyed. You can access any portion of your record at any time, simply by forming a mental affinity with it. Nothing is lost... everything is gained.

"Remember, this is still only the beginning; there is much more for you to discover.

"Time is so altered here that it barely resembles its earthly nature. Each soul is allowed however long it needs to make the full transition from the material back into the etheric realms.

"But, because of your role as a spokesman to Earth, every effort is being made to hasten your alignment. The timing is crucial, John. Earth's well-being has hung in a delicate balance since the beginning of the nuclear age."

I looked around one last time, refreshing myself with the fragrances of the valley. When I was ready to continue, Julia pointed to a small hill. Beyond it the colors were less intense... and a pale glow filled the sky.

"In the next valley we will pass through a sacred portal. No one may enter who is still connected to the denser worlds.

"The first three valleys relate to material existence. But in the fourth valley, the etheric realm will unfold in all its profound subtleties. There are no preferences of form.... We are entering the realm of pure spirit."

∞ ∞ ∞

We closed our eyes and were instantly in the fourth valley. I felt my inner vibrations heighten, and sensed a presence of extraordinary energy — but nothing could have prepared me for this next scene.

"Are these angels?" I asked. Three beings had materialized before us. Their forms were similar to mine, but with one major difference — pulsing energy was flowing out from their shoulders and then back into their bodies, creating the image of wings.

"Yes, John. Because of their direct affinity with God, angels appear to be one of His most glorious creations. They are conduits for divine nourishment, serving as links between God and the material worlds — where they are often revered as deities.

"On Earth there is a great misunderstanding concerning the angelic race. When people die and return to the etheric realms, they become more angelic *in nature*, but a human being is never transformed into an angel. Angels serve an entirely different function and purpose within the divine plan.

"These three are the Keepers of the Gate."

Transparent waves of energy radiated from the angels, much the way pavement radiates heat on a hot summer day. Projecting from their hands were brilliant streams of light filled with tiny rainbow particles. These beams formed a triangular pyramid far above our heads. As the apex grew more dense, the particles swirled within the pyramid, creating beautiful multicolored designs.

A soft, peaceful melody flowed from the brilliance, nourishing my soul. A small band of gold circled each particle, growing larger and brighter until it formed a triangle.

"The way is now clear for our passage," Mother said.

I was filled with waves of spiraling energy, feeling lighter and lighter as I flowed with the movement of the rainbow particles. The music grew louder, and it seemed my etheric body was expanding far beyond its normal size. Then the music peaked and gradually softened, leaving me peaceful and serene.

We had passed through the gate.

When I looked back the angels were gone. "Their present purpose is complete," Julia said, "but you will see them again."

It took me awhile to integrate what had just happened.

"Here in the fourth valley you will become more aware of the entire range of creative energies available to you.

"As I have said, in the etheric kingdom thoughts create instantaneous results. This is partially due to the magnetic nature of etheric substance, which is highly responsive to thought energy.

"Everything in the physical worlds is a thoughtform before it stabilizes into matter. This fourth valley acts as an electrical transformer, stepping down the energy's vibratory rate from etheric to physical frequencies. Here energy particles are condensed and focused, making them available for the creation of physical matter. When matter returns to the etheric state, the opposite takes place — the transformer steps up the vibratory rate from physical to etheric frequencies.

"This valley remains always in a non-stable condition of pure energy. Its forces are so powerful they would annihilate any dense physical matter that came into contact with them. For that reason, there is no unknown entrance, no possibility for accidental contact."

∞   ∞   ∞

The fourth valley really was different from the others. An incredible assortment of colors moved and blended rhythmically — but there were no solid forms anywhere. Nebulous patterns changed as quickly as they came together. I was wondering about the relationship between these colorforms and their physical counterparts on Earth when Mother answered my thoughts.

"What you see is the lifeforce in its free and natural state, vibrating true to its own internal frequency. The energy is no longer held within the slower bonds of matter, conforming to the vibratory needs of material worlds. It returns in joy to its original essence.

"In the fourth Temple, you will return to *your* original essence."

When the Temple appeared, its energy seemed more purified than before. The form appeared slightly out of focus — but then I realized it was fluctuating rapidly between being visible and invisible.

Mum took my hands and smiled. "You must enter alone, John. Each of us must know the truth about ourselves, for ourselves. I will wait here until you return."

A deep feeling of love welled up inside me. I knew it was a gift from my mother.

Beautiful melodies filled the air — like a master harpist was strumming the finest harp in all Creation. My soul responded with waves of elation that carried me to the entrance.

A single tone resonated from the Temple... then I was inside.

Again I felt like I'd stepped directly into the Sun. Multicolored waves of energy became a whirlwind, carrying me through complex patterns of light. I surrendered to the flow and moved faster and faster....

Then there was a blinding flash, and I was spun through an even larger design. In amazement, **I realized this was the pattern of Creation itself!**

Once I made that connection the whole pattern blended, creating a musical chord that embraced the depths of my soul. Wrapped in that blissful communion, I consciously felt the presence of God.

When the design faded I was with a being formed entirely of shimmering light waves. Light flared from its center, illuminating me with infinite love. Waves of energy swept through me so fast I almost lost awareness.

Then a ray of light flowed from my heart and merged with the light from the being. In that instant we became One.

The pulsing ray filled the interior with heavenly music — music so fascinating I didn't even notice the disappearance of the Temple.

I tried to tell Julia what had happened — but I was only beginning to understand it myself.

"Your experience in the fourth Temple has brought

nourishment to your heart and soul, even though some of it was beyond your present comprehension. Attune to your inner realities and you will know what I mean."

I realized she was right. The energy radiating from my heart was soothing my whole being. I was filled with a profound sense of peace — at last.

∞   ∞   ∞

"Know that you are God, and from that state you have become a ~~human~~ being. Eventually you will go back to your source. Do not regard God as something separate and distinct from you. God is very much within you."

Sathya Sai Baba

Three

ILLUMINATION: THE JOURNEY OF AWAKENING

"Now that the conflicts of your dual nature have been calmed," Mother said, "the etheric substance of your new form must be purified and aligned with your inner being. The fifth phase of the Temple is designed for that purpose. There you will experience the *Keeper of the Flame*."

"The Keeper of the Flame? What flame?"

"The Sacred Flame. It is a stabilization of the primordial essence of Creation," she said. "Within its intensity your alignment will be completed and you'll be prepared for the wonders still ahead.

"Things will happen very quickly in the fifth valley. If I fail to communicate fully, or if you don't understand all that happens, just be patient. Know that our Father is with us, and that everything is in divine order."

The reverence in her voice intensified my sense of awe and wonder. I was still thinking about what had happened in the fourth Temple. Things had moved pretty fast there — now she was saying they'd be moving even faster.

"The entities who will assist in your communication with

Earth are gathering now in the *Great Hall*. It is important for you to meet them as an equal."

"What is the Great Hall?" I asked. "Is it in the fifth valley?"

"The Great Hall is one of the most spectacular creations in all the etheric realms," she said. "I can't really describe it; you must experience it for yourself. But first, your seven energy centers must be aligned in the fifth Temple."

"The Sacred Flame is a direct manifestation of God's love. Within its all-consuming unity your internal conflicts will dissolve, and the full spectrum of your energies will blend into one radiant jewel.

"Again you will go in alone. Surrender your fears, your doubts, and your pain to the Sacred Flame. Surrender all your wounds, even though you may think they no longer exist. Release all limitations and open your soul to the healing balm of the Father's love. Nothing in all of Creation will nourish you so completely."

The thought of going through a fire made me a bit nervous. But Mum was so calm and reassuring... I just needed to relax. She was able to see pain in the depths of my being that I hadn't realized was there.

"The human experience is often harsh on the soul," she continued. "It wouldn't be, if those living in the physical worlds would allow the healing nourishment of God's love deeply into their hearts. When your heart fully receives that love, it begins to open and drink of the *Living Waters*. This is what Jesus meant when he spoke to the woman at the well. As you fully absorb the love of God, all your pain is finally released.

"Let's continue. The Divine Fire will illuminate any darkness that remains within you."

Those words penetrated deeply.... I knew I was being prepared for what was ahead.

∞   ∞   ∞

A web-like design of scarlet energy slowly filled the valley, increasing in brilliance at rhythmic intervals. Surrendering to the waves of energy sweeping through me, I circulated through the valley as part of the pulsing flow.

I looked at Julia and everything appeared to be standing still — but when I looked back across the valley, it was like staring into the face of eternity!

Lightning streaked across the sky. Energy crackled in midair as galaxies dispersed before my very eyes. Thousands of brilliant suns flared into one spectacular flame that expanded far beyond my awareness. I had glimpsed the reality of God's creative powers!

Julia's sweet voice centered me again. "The fifth valley is pure energy, John, much like the fourth. The differences here are primarily due to the Sacred Flame. There is no particle of Creation, even in its subatomic state, that does not contain a spark of this eternal fire. Divine light truly illuminates everything.

"Within this valley you will leave behind many of your human perceptions and begin to comprehend Creation in an entirely different way." Her eyes twinkled, and she smiled in the motherly way I remembered. "Even with all your newly-acquired knowledge and understanding, you still have a lot to learn, my dear.

"In the fifth Temple you will be prepared to behold God."

∞   ∞   ∞

Tiny globes of ruby light appeared all around us, creating tones that grew louder and louder as the brilliance of the valley intensified. Then they gathered together and, in a flash of radiant energy, fused into a single form — the fifth phase of the Temple.

"In many ways you will no longer be my son when you return from this Temple," Mother said softly. "Then you will understand our shared birthright as children of the Mother/Father God. I do love you."

"Mother, don't leave me now! I've just found you again!" I was shaken.

"Oh, my dear one, there is no force in all of Creation that could separate us now. We are united far beyond the roles of mother and son. My love for you will never diminish in any way. It goes with you now and through all eternity. I love you, John."

I held her close and whispered, "I love you too, Mother. I will always love you."

Not knowing what to expect next, I willed myself to the Temple's entrance.

This Temple looked a lot like the others, but I sensed a different kind of energy inside. There's no turning back now, I thought. So, closing my eyes, I went in.

Waves of ruby energy poured through the Temple, gradually forming a lattice-like design around me. Golden threads of light flowed freely throughout.

A single tone from the ruby globes immediately changed into a triple variation. Then, spinning rapidly, each globe divided into three smaller ones and aligned with the lattice, extending beyond my sight.

As my vibrations intensified I could hear many voices speaking at once, in languages and rhythms I didn't understand. But as I listened carefully, their meanings became clear. I realized I was hearing portions of the Earth's most treasured spiritual texts. Veil after veil lifted from my awareness, and truths that had eluded me through years of study became perfectly clear.

Suddenly the Temple filled with pulsing lights, so bright I had to shut my eyes. The lights were changing from red to vibrant pink with each flash. Then the lattice design quivered, and the energy peaked in a climactic surge.

An enormous fiery being stood before me! As the internal lighting shifted, I could see the full spectrum of the rainbow glowing within its form.

There were no features I could recognize, but its powerful energies were focused on me as though I were being studied under a microscope. Then, through some metamorphosis I didn't understand, it transformed into a gigantic flame of indescribable beauty.

Radiating waves of energy, the flame expanded until I was consumed within its brilliance. One by one, different colors emerged, stimulating dramatic changes in my energy centers.

My mind ignited with the fire of a million suns, as images and energies blended into one inseparable whole. The very substance of my etheric body was altered and purified.

I was standing face-to-face with Creation... free of all mental limitations and consumed with ecstatic joy.

Finally all that remained was the flame, burning pure and bright and showing no trace of any color. Then it slowly faded — leaving only the memory of its existence.

The Temple had vanished and Mother was by my side. As I poured out the images of what had happened, I was surprised at my new ability to communicate so freely.

"Your capacity to relate with all of Creation will continue to grow," she said. "As children of God — made in His image — we are each a reflection of all that He is."

∞   ∞   ∞

"Let's continue the journey, John. There are many who await us in the Great Hall. Stand close and I will guide you."

An odd assortment of images passed through my mind in the instant it took to get there — but they moved by so fast I didn't recognize most of them.

We were now in a more earthlike setting. Surrounding the Hall was a beautiful garden, but it scarcely caught my eye — the energy radiating from the Hall was so intense I could focus on little else.

It seemed to be made from layers of multicolored light, and

was somehow less dense than the other etheric structures I'd seen. Spires of energy were soaring far up into the distance.

"This is a great privilege," Julia said. "The beauty of this sacred place truly enriches the soul. Shall we enter and share in the abundance of divine truth?"

I stepped back, attempting to drink in the magnificent splendor of the Hall. Then I turned to Mother. "I'm ready. Let's go in."

The sound of an angelic choir filled the ethers, and an opening appeared in the wall before us. I felt powerfully energized.

A transparent golden sphere formed around us and we entered the Great Hall, moving through a sea of shimmering energy.

"John, this sphere is vibrationally aligned with the beings who await us — it will take us to them.

"All of Creation is represented within this Hall. Its true immensity is beyond our comprehension, for it blends with realms where space, as we have known it, does not exist. We could happily travel within this treasure house for eternity, but we will visit only the area where our meeting is to take place."

The sphere slowed and the swirling colors cleared, revealing a room of huge proportions. It was filled with books and scrolls of every imaginable size and color.

"These volumes contain the wisdom of the ages," Julia said. "Every race that has ever existed in any of the manifest worlds, and all the knowledge the Mind has ever encountered, are recorded here.

"All the founders of Earth's great religions have visited this room. Some came consciously, while others had more symbolic encounters. The effects were always the same — they recognized the divinity of humanity and attempted to reveal this truth to the people in ways that suited their individual times and personal understandings.

"No one can come here solely for personal benefit. Only those who are aware of their unity with Creation can enter the Great Hall."

"That sounds like a fairly simple requirement," I said.

"But to many it would be the most complex problem they have ever encountered," she responded. "Most of those living in the finite worlds are not aware of their unity with God. They are conscious of their bodies, but have little understanding of their souls.

"The soul is eternal. It is God's manifestation into our personal reality. **Souls live in constant communion with God, and are living extensions of His essence**. In truth, the separation that humanity has imagined does not exist.

"Let's go on. Many of those who wait for us have spent lifetimes on Earth serving God and humanity. You will recognize some of them, but most are from other time periods.

"Earth has provided a home for many races, most of which are unfamiliar to modernday humanity. Regardless of our apparent differences, we are all united in the Creator's love."

∞ ∞ ∞

As the sound of the choir returned, the vibrations around our sphere intensified, and again we moved through the glistening sea of energy. I knew we would soon reach our destination — a sacred space deep within the Great Hall.

In an explosion of color we penetrated the interior. Our sphere began to rotate rapidly, then suddenly stopped as its walls dissolved in a flash of violet light.

The incredible beauty around us was almost overwhelming. I could see what had inspired the creation of Earth's great Cathedrals. Mum seemed as amazed as I was.

"Do you know where we are?" I asked.

"This is the *Sanctuary of the Angels*. I know very few details, but I've heard that the angels come here when they are involved in the highest aspects of divine service. You have been called here because the work planned for you will be of great benefit to mankind."

We stood on a floor of constantly changing and interlocking colors. Columns of energy soared up beyond my sight, and somehow I knew they joined in great arches high overhead. The harmonies of the choir filled the Sanctuary, energizing the columns and intensifying their colors.

A golden mist slowly formed around us.

"Many who have come to meet you laid aside their etheric forms long ago. In preparation for this meeting, they have temporarily clothed themselves in etheric substance to relate and communicate with you more clearly."

While she was speaking, the mist had condensed into several hundred separate forms, most of them equal in size to my own. Gradually they became more solid, until I could no longer see through any of them. Then a face appeared on each one, as though a master sculptor had passed among them. I recognized several, but most were unknown to me.

"These entities are capable of providing the specific nourishment and guidance Earth needs at this time," she said. "Some represent other realms, but most are of the Earth's vibration. The Father has assembled the perfect energies for this task, including yours, my dear. They will introduce themselves and give you a review of their work."

As we moved among them I was filled with awe and humility, realizing the Creator was speaking through each of these souls. I stood among beings of saintly purity and wisdom, yet somehow I knew I belonged. I was starting to understand the significance of this meeting — what we were gathering to achieve would impact the entire human race.

The beings blended their frequencies with ours, forming a sea of energy. No longer held within separate forms, we shared the depths of our souls and became totally unified. In the radiance of that communion no form was left visible — I felt a presence of ecstasy more profound than words can describe.

Then a voice spoke from the mist. "Within the light we are One."

Her voice had such a refreshing purity — unlike anything I'd ever heard. The essence of love in her words embraced my soul, and I felt like I'd just awakened from a deep sleep. It seemed like I was always awakening here.

"I greet you in the name of the Creator, sweet child of light. I rejoice at your participation in this display of God's love. Humanity must realize that God *is* love and that love is the source of all Creation — indeed all life.

"God is the living bond that binds us together as one being. Within this union there is no separation, no loss, no death — only love and eternal life.

"Every aspect of Creation is in a state of preparation, but *our* focus is to prepare the Earth. This is what your mother spoke of as 'divine intervention in the human experience.' Humanity must be made ready to receive what the Creator has to share.

"In times of greatest need, the Divine Force has always intervened in the affairs of man; and so it is again. The Creator will not allow Earth to be destroyed, for that world has yet to serve the true purpose for which it was created."

The music of her voice lingered in my mind after the sound of her words had faded.

"Listen well, John," Mother said. "This one has counseled many souls and enlightened many minds. She is in complete resonance with the Living Waters — in complete harmony with the soothing vibrations of God's love. Therefore, she will serve as the focal point for this gathering.

"In preparation for your communication with Earth, you will soon return to the unified awareness you experienced earlier. Even now you are recording these events for our people.

"Because of the nature of the message you will deliver to

Earth, it was essential that your transition occur in a manner which preserved the clarity of your awareness. This is why you bypassed many of the normal events of crossing over. That clarity will be vital to our endeavors.

"Aspects of this meeting are being altered so the details and the information shared will be easier for mankind to understand."

"What do you mean by *altered*?" I asked.

"I'll give you a direct example. The loving being who just spoke did not do so as an individual. Everyone here merged telepathically to speak through her with one voice."

"So that explains the unique quality of her voice," I said.

"It is the blending of all those here, as well as her own internal purity, that makes her voice so special," Julia replied. "You will hear it again, but now three others are here to share their wisdom with you."

Three entities appeared, radiating waves of crystalline energy. As a ray of gold from the center being fused with my essence, I heard a deep, resonant voice.

"We greet you in the name of the Creator. We three were privileged to assist in designing the physical body through which the soul travels in the material worlds.

"The physical body is called the Temple of the Soul, for the soul is the only element that directly receives the complete current of divine love. This current nourishes the soul while it is clothed in the dense matter of physical substance.

"When the divine current ceases to flow from the soul into the body's receiving stations (chakras), its physical form is shed.

The soul's departure from the body is what humanity calls death.

"The soul is a jewel beyond compare, and the physical vehicle through which it expresses on Earth is an intricate balance of energies that almost defies comprehension. To those who can see the invisible spectrum, the body is a brilliant creation of design and color.

"The physical form is empowered by the soul. The seven etheric bodies serve as electrical transformers which step down the divine energy to frequencies the physical body can safely accept as nourishment. The etheric bodies also stabilize the soul's vibration within Earth's energy flow.

"Each etheric body has a receiving and transmitting center that interacts with the entire network of energy flowing through the unified structure.[1] These centers also receive energy from Earth's seven frequency levels.

"One of the purposes of this gathering is to inform humanity of the soul's true nature. Until people fully understand the soul, the nature of life will remain a mystery.

"Souls live and breathe within the Heart of God. They may manifest in the external worlds thousands of times, but souls never completely leave the etheric kingdom. Through this eternal connection, God lives in each one of us, as each of us lives within God.

"The energies surrounding the soul are what some people see as patterns of light and color in the aura. What appears to be

---

1. The soul, the etheric bodies and the physical body.

a spirit body surrounding the physical form is actually multiple layers of atomic and subatomic particles magnetically aligned with the etheric bodies. These layers blend the etheric frequencies with Earth's primary vibration. Without this insulation, the powerful vibrations from the etheric bodies would cause the complete dissolution of Earth."

That sounded pretty far-out. "How could that be?" I asked.

The ray connecting us deepened in color, radiating spirals of golden energy as the voice continued. "You will understand after you have gone through the last phases of the Temple. Your education concerning many aspects of Creation is incomplete, so we will explain further.

"Humans will be able to communicate with all levels of existence when they fully understand the relationship between their physical and etheric bodies.

"Physical bodies are formed through the interaction of etheric bodies with various particles and energies surrounding Earth. When we speak of energy, we refer to the *substance* of Creation. Atomic and subatomic particles are simply energy, vibrating at different frequencies to create larger physical elements.

"Five major energy currents blend to create the primary chord of Earth's vibration. When the seven etheric bodies are interwoven with these energy currents, a balance is achieved in which the human body can be created and sustained. This vibrational orchestration is unsurpassed within the whole of Creation.

"A vast network of interrelated transmission and connection points coordinates all of these vibrations. The magnetic quality of the soul is the cohesive force that stabilizes this alignment. When a soul leaves the physical body at death, this stabilization no longer exists and the body begins to disintegrate.

"Balanced within this network is a secondary response system which supplements the function of the chakras. Eight additional transmission centers are each surrounded by eight smaller centers. This system continually alters and aligns the soul's energy to blend within the frequencies of Earth.

"In order for balance to be maintained, all energies within this system must pass through each of these points and many smaller points. This process is reversed at death to disconnect and release the etheric bodies.

"One of the primary reasons we are all gathered here is to assist your people in reaching a complete balance within this immense range of vibrations."

"Some people on Earth sense a divine influence in every aspect of earthly activity; they will respond to the love we are sending forth. Many who remember you as a spokesman for world peace will welcome you as such again."

The connecting ray faded as the message ended. Golden energy radiated from all three beings and their forms lost focus in the brilliance. When the light dimmed, they had taken their places among the multitude in the Sanctuary.

∞   ∞   ∞

"Humanity is now moving into an age of increasing emancipation from many of its past limitations. Technical achievements and medical advances confer growing freedom from various oppressions and ills. Man's greatest problem is still himself and his orientation to his fellow-beings. To understand himself fully he must become aware of the fact that he does not consist merely of a temporary form which is doomed to age and die. He has an immortal soul which is housed in an immortal body and endowed with a mind that is independent of the physical brain."

Sir Donald Tovey

Four

HUMANITY: THE BRIDGE BETWEEN HEAVEN AND EARTH

I stood quietly in the stillness of the Sanctuary, feeling a deep sense of unity. So much about life had been explained since I left Earth. It was clear that this gathering perfectly represented the entire range of human experience.

I was exploring these realizations when Julia spoke again.

"I said before that your affinity with the millions on Earth who admired you and loved your music is our strongest line of transmission. Because your essential connection with humanity was through music, an entity who was a master musician on Earth is here to share his wisdom with you."

Violet light surrounded the form that appeared. His face was slightly veiled by the light, but I could feel his infinite kindness and wisdom.

A ray of gold connected his form with mine, and I received a flow of music so beautiful and nurturing I could have listened forever. An endless variety of rhythms and melodies blended and reblended. Familiar passages would surface, but as soon as I recognized a pattern, it changed into something entirely new and different.

Then the music started forming speech patterns — giving birth to a voice that reminded me of running water. It was a trickling stream of sounds with a soothing, peaceful quality all its own.

"I greet you in the name of the Creator — and in remembrance of all we have shared."

He flared brilliantly and the ray of energy connecting us pulsed with a fascinating display of colors. My mind flooded with memories of life on Earth — and *before*. I became aware of my presence *before* I took an earthly form! The assortment of energies surrounding me then was very similar to the energies of this gathering.

I remembered the vow I'd made before my life on Earth began — and realized every part of it was coming true.

"Now that our internal frequencies are resonating in alignment, we are truly in remembrance of all we have shared.

"Your mother summoned me many times to help you with your musical creativity. Other etheric sources also contributed to your work so it would have meaning for a broader spectrum of people than is usual for any one segment of music. Our messages of love and peace are most easily conveyed through the universal medium of music.

"Music is the language of the Creator. The primary vibration of the Creator gave birth to the initial motion that generates all form. Rhythm is the universal law of divine motion and is the basic guide for all music.

"Rhythm is also the language of life. From the time a soul takes a human form, until it returns to the etheric realms, it is constantly seeking to be nourished by this rhythm — and through that nourishment, to obtain perfect balance.

"The etheric bodies surrounding the soul are intricately blended with the energies that form the physical body. More intricate still is the balancing of these vibrations into a single frequency in harmony with the soul's primary vibration.

"People on Earth have waited æons to achieve this blissful state of unified resonance. Our focus is to assist in its creation.

"Much is being done on many levels to help humans expand their awareness of the etheric realms. Other groups are working in separate ways and through different channels — all unified within the Divine Plan. Our contribution is only one of the final sequences in an extended effort to achieve a single balanced frequency.

"Humans must realize that the physical body is only a small part of their nature. The fragmentation people experience is caused by thoughts of separation from God.

"They will learn what you have learned: **the physical body and the entire material realm exist only in relation to the soul**.

"As souls continue to unfold, the physical worlds will respond with greater degrees of harmony and clarity. The people on Earth have now evolved enough to *consciously* benefit from our assistance. We will focus much of that assistance through you, John. The world remembers what you have given, but the gifts you have yet to give are even more important."

∞   ∞   ∞

The master musician was really an extraordinary teacher. Light years flashed between the levels of my comprehension as streams of information poured into my soul.

Images formed and reformed in a vast panorama of light, until I lost all sense of time and space. Like foam cascading from a fountain, I fell through an explosion of stars... and experienced the infinite ocean of eternity.

Moving swiftly across the face of Earth, I witnessed coming events. What mankind has achieved throughout history is almost nothing compared to the quantum leap it is about to experience. **Earth's destiny is a total embrace of the miraculous.**

∞   ∞   ∞

The master musician continued speaking of many things, seen and unseen....

"Beings from other levels of existence have laid the foundation for our communication by grounding a greater capacity for receptivity within Earth's electrical fields. Many have gone before you, preparing the people to receive our gifts.

"The people of Earth are interwoven with the planet through a blending of their vibratory nature — from the atom to the soul — with Earth's electrical fields. This blending enables them to live within the electrical realities of that world.

"A portion of our focus is to educate people about this electrical relationship and how it can help them reach their full potential. But first they must understand the nature of their formation and existence on Earth."

Again I felt the impact this gathering would have on the world I had so recently left... and my feelings of reverence deepened.

The three architects of the human body suddenly reappeared and, with a unified consciousness, continued their communication.

"Humans need to understand the nature of their bodies and the balance of energies that allows them to be created. We are here as a specific aspect of Divine Mind to fulfill this need.

"**The human race is a bridge between essence and form — between Heaven and Earth.** When a being is clothed in a physical body, the soul forms a bridge between the physical and etheric realms.

"Within the human cell all realities merge. Matter and antimatter converge in rhythmic movement, allowing energies to blend and focus — achieving one of the most intricate balances in all of Creation.

"Every physical manifestation, including Earth, is a stabilization of energies projected from the Divine Source. The *Primary Matrix* is a focal point of stabilized energies within the planet. All lifeforms on Earth are harmonized with this Matrix, resulting in their compatible coexistence. Solar radiation is the key vibration that harmonizes the various lifeforms into one cohesive system.

"We are now completing the process of blending the human consciousness with the consciousness of Earth. **Then humanity and Earth will experience and express their divine destiny together.**"

Struck by the impact of this revelation, I spiraled upward in an incredible outpouring of energy. As I absorbed the wonders of the Sanctuary deeply into my being, I understood why this majestic place was chosen for our gathering. Its beauty perfectly reflects the Divine Presence flowing through the core of the angelic host as the source of its creativity.

The architects continued.

"Again we remind you — this gathering does not work alone in these activities. Many divine agencies are united in this focusing of light.

"One of our greatest revelations to humanity is that **the very ethers are alive** and vibrating in response to the Divine Presence.

"Divine light sweeps through the nucleus of every atom at such great speed that humanity is literally woven, faster than the speed of light, into the very fabric of Creation. When humans understand this, they will have a much greater appreciation for the nature of their own existence.

"Humanity's infinite capacity to communicate comes through an alignment between the seven frequency levels within the Earth's Primary Matrix and the seven energy fields within the atom.

"Within the nucleus of the atom is an eighth energy field, which is the attuned combination of the other seven. This is also true of the Primary Matrix. Each energy field in the atom is individually tuned to its corresponding frequency within the Matrix."

∞ ∞ ∞

It took a bit for me to understand all these relationships.

"The Sanctuary of the Angels is a vortex of inflowing divine nourishment through which God embraces His Creation," Julia said. "One of our jobs is to help people understand and accept the unlimited care and love with which they are being served."

"John, you must pass through the *Veil of Light* and experience the Presence within the sixth phase of the Temple. This is essential, not only to your own completion, but for the broader scope of our activities in the Sanctuary."

In a powerful surge of energy I spiraled upward again — only this time I was joined by two angelic beings. They looked different from the other angels I'd seen. Delicate patterns of violet and purple pulsed from the center of their bodies, flowing out as two majestic wings. Each had a band of gold light around its forehead, and communicated by flashing light pulses from these bands. It was fascinating.

"Be at peace. We come before you as servants of your own divine being to form a bond between the aspect that was your earthly identity as 'John,' and the infinite reality of your soul. Through this bond a resonance will be maintained with Earth until your communication is complete.

"A transition will now enfold your soul, so that you may know the full expression of its creative light."

As the angels radiated flashes of violet, the energy from their thoughtforms expanded within me. Then, in an explosion of violet energy, the gathering of beings and the Great Hall disappeared.

∞   ∞   ∞

The two angels accompanied me into the sixth valley. Great waves of energy moved through the violet mist, illumined by golden spheres of light.

By raising their vibratory rate, the angels created a pure and penetrating tone that grew louder as the spheres expanded. Then, creating an incredibly exhilarating music, the spheres fused together in an explosion of golden light. It was the sixth Temple of the Octave.

Violet columns created a spectacular opalescent form similar to the first five Temples — but even more beautiful. A ray of purple light flared from the interior, and I was immediately inside.

Embraced by the Presence, I felt a surge of ecstasy so powerful that I lost all sense of separateness.

Aspects of the first five Temples materialized before me in rapid succession. Intricate patterns of energy were alive with the diamond "fireflies" I'd seen in the second Temple. Creating a soft, soothing music, they swarmed around me until I was encased in a sphere of diamond light.

As the sphere moved through shimmering liquid toward a cobalt-blue orb, a single tone vibrated my essence with such power I thought I would dissolve. Instead, a ray of gold encased in deep blue flared from my sphere into the center of the orb, and the single tone became a celestial rhapsody! Wave after wave of joyous harmony swirled around me, building up to a final brilliant crescendo of gold and cobalt.

I flew through the complex patterns of the orb into a whirlpool of rainbow-colored energy. Surrendering completely, I was pulled through its center into a sparkling diamond cone.

A burst of clear white light pushed me through the apex of the cone, and I was transformed into *living light*. I experienced Creation from a profoundly different perspective — not as an observer, but as the *Source*.

Time and space merged into one vast pulsating design. Universes rippled like ocean waves, creating new realities in great flashes of light. Mirror images of universes reflected back, allowing the Light to comprehend Itself. Matter and antimatter whirled in shared waves, sparkling with the fluid movement of divine radiance. Interlocking realms combined in immense pulsations of light, while dimensions of pure spirit fused with matter in the expressive dance of Divine Mind.

∞   ∞   ∞

A stirring of activity brought me back to an individual awareness. My two violet friends reappeared briefly to calm me, then were gone again.

One by one the beings from the first five Temples materialized in brilliant bursts of color. As the last one faded, an extraordinary presence filled the ethers. Again I soared upward in a spiral of energy, whirling faster and faster in the golden light.

When the movement stopped I was back in the sixth

Temple. It had become a dazzling reflection of rainbow-colored prisms.

A golden form surged from the brilliance, and the ethers vibrated with this message: "Behold the light. Behold, I am in you... and you are in me."

In a series of light pulses the being continued: "I create this form as a reflection of our unity. I will reveal Divine Mind to you, that you may record these truths.

"The form before you now is the first of three I shall create to convey this revelation. As you embrace my reality, I will expand my light so you can behold me more clearly.

"Behold, I am all time and all space. I am the rhythm of the moving universes of light. I am the infinite wave of divine activity.

"Behold our unity. Remind your people of our eternal equality. All of Creation is unified within the radiance of my divine light.

"Reveal to the people the true nature of *their* divine light. They are not limited, material beings as they now believe, but are sacred expressions of my divine nature. Have them remove these limiting concepts from their minds, that they may be filled with the nourishment of my vitality.

"Every aspect of Creation is sustained and anointed with my divine presence. The full experience of my love is withheld from no one. Reveal to your people the infinite sustaining quality of this love.

"**All things, from the smallest unit of stabilized light, which your race perceives as matter, to the most complex frequency alignment — the human brain and central nervous**

system — are simply aspects of Divine Being. So it is with the whole of Creation. Your people must now understand this. The Earth is nurtured completely through the rhythmic embrace of divine love.

"Behold, I am the womb of light from which all Creation is born. I am the door to the Kingdom. I am the spiral of light that embraces you as you enter and exit the various realms of Creation.

"Many have been my messengers in the manifest worlds. You, my child, are an aspect of myself through which I now embrace your planet in this moment of unity. Go forth as a ray of Divine Presence, and know that those who will assist you on Earth have been well chosen.

"I am the embrace of light."

The sixth Temple vanished as the being's final words resonated within me.

∞   ∞   ∞

My light body merged with a spiral of blue-white energy, and I realized the entire gathering from the Sanctuary had filled its interior! Their energy fused with the spiral, transforming it into a magnificent jewel of diamond light.

Realms parted before the energy wave of our spiral, and I was amazed to see radiant beings throughout the vastness of space. Several were attracted to our light and blended their energies with ours — creating waves of joy and fantastic displays of color.

Throughout these exchanges I was being drawn toward the

apex of the spiral. Just before reaching it, I heard my mother: "John, I am with you in the joy of this moment. Together we are flowing within the essence of the divine embrace to share our light with humanity.

"Now, as you fuse with the apex, you will blend with the beings in this spiral as well as with the man who waits on Earth for your contact. This will be the final link in a bridge of light extended through time and space to embrace our planet."

I fused with the apex of the spiral and realized Mother was sharing a personal blending with me and with God. In that moment I was anointed with divine light.

∞   ∞   ∞

The powerful waves of energy in the spiral caused a portion of my essence to extend beyond the apex. As I contacted and blended with the Earth's essence, a surge of golden light engulfed the spiral and embraced the planet. This quickened the Earth's Primary Matrix, grounding it within the frequency of the light wave.

Rhythmic pulsations of color joined with my energy as I flew through the Earth's auric designs. My soul was being fine-tuned to the vibrations of the Matrix. Endless streams of information flowed into my mind while Earth shared the secrets of her divine nature. Then, at the fastest rate Earth's vibratory nature would allow, I soared through the complex array of patterns forming the Matrix.

Layer after layer of energy patterns opened before me like the petals of a heavenly flower. As I moved into the core of the

Matrix, I was instantly inside an immense golden crystal — the seventh Temple of the Octave.

A spinning column of light radiated diamond energy as the Presence of the Temple flowed into my essence. In that embrace I shared a true communion with divine light.

"Behold the light. Within the light we are One.

"Behold, my child, as the lightwave embraces your planet. The bridge has been formed, and the one chosen to receive your communion stands ready.

"Behold Earth in this moment of her transformation. The magnificence of our embrace flows out into eternity through the infinity of space.

"I am the light of the Earth."

One crystal-clear note penetrated my essence, and I was momentarily drawn back into the Matrix. As I whirled through its brilliant design, vast etheric regions revealed their hidden life forms.

∞   ∞   ∞

Then I was back in the Sanctuary, embraced again by the Divine Presence.

"Behold, I am the infinite wave of divine activity. I am the light you now focus. I am the transformation of the Earth."

A column of violet energy appeared beside me, and I was astonished when it transformed into my mother! "John, through the infinite compassion and wisdom of the Divine

Presence, I come to you in form this last time to remind you of my eternal love. I release you into the essence of the light that you are. Anoint our world with your light as you assist in its transformation.

"**Our race is an entity of light which even now transcends the limits of the past and embraces the infinite possibilities of the moment.** You are a child of light. Go forth with courage in the assurance of that light."

Then, in a brilliant flash, my mother became one with Creation.

∞ ∞ ∞

"When science begins the study of non-physical phenomena, it will make more progress in one decade than in all the centuries of its existence."

NIKOLA TESLA

Five
THE FOUNTAIN OF LIGHT

"The embrace of light has heightened Earth's frequencies. As the Primary Matrix becomes attuned to these higher vibrations, the planet will be ready to receive the energies focused from this Sanctuary."

The two violet angels had joined our gathering. Their golden headbands pulsed with the information they were transmitting.

"Great centers of light have been created at *node points* within the Primary Matrix. Beings from Earth's seven realms of light are weaving their energies into the Matrix at these node points and directing their combined focus into its core.

"Within the Primary Matrix, alterations have begun that will restructure the nature and activity of every lifeform on Earth.

"Any frequency which alters the Matrix changes the entirety of Earth — from the bodies of her physical lifeforms to the very purpose of her being. When the adjustments are complete, only those lifeforms that continue to harmonize with the new Primary Matrix can remain; all others will be transported to realms more suited to their needs.

"Earth's primary lifeform, the human race, is prepared to remain with the planet, but it must undergo many alterations as it synchronizes its frequency with the new Matrix."

I was hungry for details. I cared so deeply....

"Your planet has served many great souls, just as she now serves the Collective Human Soul. Your people aligned with Earth æons ago in preparation for this experience, for the Soul can see far beyond the boundaries of time and space."

"After your transformation in the eighth Temple, we will focus our light through you to anoint the Earth. In preparation for this transmission, immense portals of light are being opened to bathe the Earth in divine radiance. Earth is destined to transcend the *Primary Light Threshold*[1] and align with a group of stars not yet perceived by humanity.

"Invisible beams of ultra-high-frequency light are being projected along intricate grid patterns to ensure Earth's correct orientation within the new star grouping."

This *really* made me curious....

∞   ∞   ∞

"Earth is deeply loved and cared for, and all her people as well. Divine love is the source of these changes, sustaining the

---

1. A built-in vibratory resistance in the optic nerve which prevents the passage of frequencies above those of the primary light code. Presently, the "normal" optic nerve can perceive only the frequencies of the primary light code.

planet and nourishing the many light beings who serve her. Love is the living light that sustains the ethers — the infinite flow of Life manifesting. **Love is transforming the Earth.**"

"The Collective Human Soul is transcending into a higher frequency. *New codes of sequential phasing* will enable individual human souls to adjust their energy bodies into a unified field of light awareness — so they can *consciously* participate in the Collective Mind.

"We have much information to share with your people concerning these alterations. As the entire universe joins to support the transformation, Earth is stimulating ancient energies within her Primary Matrix to quicken the lightpulse of her being."

"Increased energy exchanges between the realms of light and key node points within the Matrix will accelerate great changes in the Earth's exterior form.

"The Collective Human Soul will respond to these exchanges by transmuting many of its limiting thoughtforms. This will convert every level of the human form into a higher frequency."

I could think of a few limiting thoughtforms I had tried to change while on Earth... war, for instance.

A sudden imprint of energy caused a knowing within me about the changes underway.... And my consciousness soared!

Time and space dissolved. All of Creation ceased to exist as I floated blissfully in a sea of crystal-clear energy. Experiencing the clear light of my own essence, I was transformed in a state of profound ecstasy.

I knew this ecstatic experience would happen for each person on Earth. Everyone would be going through an individual transformation as profound as my own.

∞   ∞   ∞

Seven radiant geometric energy forms appeared before me. A burst of iridescent rainbow light created an eighth form, and I was immediately drawn into its center — the eighth and final phase of the Temple.

I sensed a Presence vibrating at the highest frequency I had yet experienced. My own frequency altered to align with this Presence and, in a brilliant flash of light, it flowed into my being.

"Behold the light. Within the light we are One.

"Through the creativity of my love, I have allowed these two aspects of myself — my presence and your light essence — to exist momentarily within a balanced, rhythmic exchange of light.

"I am the rhythmic exchange of light.

"I am the radiant symphony of the ethers. The eternal vibration of my divine love is the sound that echoes through the vastness of space. As light moves within my mind, sound is created throughout the universe. You have vibrated with those sounds as you experienced the various realms of light.

"I am the infinite wave of divine activity. My presence rhythmically aligns the energy that forms the universes moving through time and space.

"I am the vast legions of stellar beings who illuminate and nourish the denser worlds.

"I am the living revelation of light. I reveal to your people the nature of light and the infinite range of frequencies that allows them to experience my Creation.

"As the frequencies of Earth change, her stellar orientation alters. Great stellar beings are aligning with her new vibration, bringing with them the winds of change for your planet.

"Behold, as I anoint the Earth with divine radiance. In the language of light I create a vibration of harmony and joy, and cause it to flow into the Earth.

"Behold, as Earth attunes to these light pulsations, blending their energies into the brilliant prism of her Primary Matrix.

"I summoned the gathering in the Sanctuary to blend the light energy of this revelation into the Collective Mind of your race, and to align the frequency of the Mind with that of the Primary Matrix."

∞   ∞   ∞

I had become a conscious energy flow coursing through the dazzling intricacies of the Matrix. A focused ray of energy flowed through me from the Sanctuary, and I knew that our transmission to Earth had begun.

In a burst of soft gold energy a sudden transformation took place. The Matrix blossomed into the first of the geometric energy forms that had escorted me into the clear light of the eighth Temple. As this energy form embraced Earth, I realized our planet was entering the phase shift sequence the Divine Being had spoken of. Earth had begun the initial stages of fusing the seven realms of her Matrix into one cohesive, unified system.

I was vibrating with the impact of these realizations when the two violet angels reappeared.

"John, once again we enfold you within our presence. Through the combination of our energies, we will strengthen and complete the alignment between Earth and the gathering in the Sanctuary.

"Soon you will return, for they have more to share with you. But now, just as Earth embraces the transformation within her Primary Matrix, you must embrace the completion of your healing."

I found myself whirling at a fantastic speed through the transformed Matrix. An array of green crystalline points of light transmission pulsed in perfect unison, as the angels continued to share their wisdom:

"Earth must know and experience unity as an internal condition, as well as an external reality. Once all the kingdoms of light that exist in harmony with Earth commune with one another, a deeper realization of their common source will unify them as one kingdom. Then the stellar realms will unite with Earth and *the heavens will no longer be distant.*"

"Unity will cleanse your planet and create a world of total harmony, peace, and love."

The Primary Matrix changed into the second geometric energy form. Streams of images poured through me as the transmission to Earth continued. Light beings from the second realm responded by soaring around the planet, projecting their radiance back into the transformed Matrix through glistening aquamarine prisms.

"These light beings are imprinted with celestial energy that is now being released into Earth's electrical fields," my two violet friends explained. "Your planet holds many treasures deep within her being — the time has come for her to bring these treasures forth."

As the Matrix transformed into the third geometric form, Earth's light created a fantastic design of deep cobalt blue. Silver light from the Sanctuary flowed through me into the Matrix, triggering a sequence of golden-cobalt pulsations. A series of three clear, penetrating tones repeated three times.

I saw a spiral of beings bringing gifts of light and love from the infinity of space. Untold numbers of light beings were entering through the third realm to minister to the denser nature of Earth.

Next, a rapid series of ruby pulsations changed the Primary Matrix into the fourth geometric form. A maze of lattices pulsed with golden light as violet energy surged through the design. Light poured through me into the center of the Matrix, imprinting a complex code of deep violet sparks.

Light beings flowed from the Matrix and gathered around the planet, transmitting a variation of the violet code to node points in the fourth energy form.

∞   ∞   ∞

Then, spirals of amber energy transformed the Matrix into the fifth geometric form. Electric-blue lightning bolts sparked from its center, revealing the enormous power that animates the Earth.

Huge electric-blue beings swirled through the core of the Matrix, quickening and sustaining Earth's essence. I experienced with them the reality of Earth's transformation and shared the joy my race will soon know. To witness the awakening of a dreaming entity such as Earth is cause for great celebration. Many beings were coming from the far reaches of space to join the party.

The Primary Matrix changed again — into the sixth energy form. Clear white light flared from its center, etching a diamond design and then weaving it back into the form. Then it started to vibrate, and a procession of rainbow beings emerged from its center. Forming into groups, they projected beams of various colors into specific regions of the Matrix.

The violet angels were with me again.

"These children of light are transmitting energy from the

sixth realm to light beings within the second. The two groups work together in precise alignment, adjusting celestial energy to the vibratory needs of Earth.

"The sixth realm will provide a vital service by assisting in the healing, revitalization, and transmutation of humanity — the seventh realm of Earth."

A jolt of energy from the Sanctuary surged through me, creating a diamond light around the Matrix as it transformed into the seventh geometric form.

Endless images and thoughtforms flowed through my consciousness. The Earth receives such profound care from the beings who serve her — and I was thrilled to be one of them!

The two violet angels reappeared. "Many aspects of human nature remain undiscovered and unexplored. Soon your people will realize the infinite nature of their being and participate in the wondrous transformation now embracing their planetary home.

"Inspire them to love and bless Earth as the sacred entity that she is.

"Awaken humanity to the wonder of this moment."

The Matrix blossomed into a sparkling pulsation of diamond light, and I was drawn into its center. My body was vibrating intensely. The powerful energy flowing through me seemed to dissolve all form and space.

Then the Divine Presence was with me again.

"Behold the light."

My light essence transformed into a shining version of the

man I had been on Earth. A fountain of glistening energy flowed from the ethers, bathing me in its radiance.

"Peace, my child; within the light we are One. Enter this light and be One with me."

Without hesitation I entered the Fountain of Light. The Divine Presence took on a shimmering form and joined me — we were completely embraced by the energy flow of the fountain.

The Presence stilled my energy with a touch to my forehead, then directed a ray of clear light into each chakra. A vast assortment of images and energies flowed through me, and when the ray entered my heart center, I experienced the imagery sequence of my own death.

As these pictures faded, I felt the presence of my two sons. One sweet moment of remembrance — and they were gone.

"Behold the light of my divine love.

"Behold, I am the ever-moving wave of divine activity. I am, indeed, all Life."

The energy of those words expanded within me. I experienced the living universes of light, where worlds of every description dance through the infinity of space.

"Behold the sustaining nature of my compassion. Experience the vitality of my being, and allow my eternal joy to quicken within you.

"My presence sustains Creation within the infinite lightwave of my eternal being. Throughout the realms of time and space — I AM. Remind those you now serve that *within the light we are One.*"

Then in a great burst of light, the Divine Being and the fountain were gone.

∞   ∞   ∞

"All our science measured against reality is primitive and childlike."

ALBERT EINSTEIN

Six
THE BODY ELECTRIC

A SURGE OF JOYOUS ENERGY WELCOMED ME BACK TO THE Sanctuary. The bond unifying me with this divine company of beings was even deeper now that our transmission had begun.

The three architects of the human form reappeared.

"John, the energy focused through you has quickened the Earth, triggering a complete transformation within the Primary Matrix. This will allow her to unite the various realms of her being.

"The energy now being transmitted from the Matrix is stimulating the ethers within Earth's solar system to reveal her unseen companions. As the solar system expands, so does the number of frequency levels that can be experienced and expressed on Earth. The visual spectrum is unfolding to embrace these higher frequencies of light. No longer will your people be blinded to the radiant spectrum of life surrounding them.

"Just as we have served the Earth, we will now serve humanity — her primary race. On each planet, members of the primary race have the inherent ability to manifest the entirety of Divine Presence within their beings. Once this ability is consciously realized, they have complete access to the infinite realms of Creation. Having been 'made in the image of God,' **the only restrictions humans have are those they impose upon themselves.**"

I wondered how many people would be able to handle that concept.

"Every aspect of human activity influences your planet. What you term 'civilization' has always been interwoven with Earth's transformations. Your people have not only altered the Earth by their presence, but they have been altered by her as well — and so it will continue.

"In alignment with this mutual transformation, and in harmony with the energy our gathering has transmitted into the Primary Matrix, we now call forth within the human race a deeper understanding and realization of its true nature.

"As we transmit light through you into the energy field of your race, light codes magnetically sealed within the human cellular structure will be released into the physical tissues. These light codes will remove the illusion of separation that has entranced the majority of your people. As they comprehend their purpose and perfection, the fears that have enslaved them will evaporate within the light of their own radiance."

The three architects moved closer, and a wave of energy swept through my light body as the entire gathering formed a circle around the four of us.

"The human body is an intricate and highly sensitive electrical instrument," they continued. "It is designed to receive and transmit vibrations of various frequencies — a vehicle for the soul's experience and expression in the physical worlds.

"Most of your people have perceived themselves only as physical forms, clothed for a moment within a world that seems distant and separate. Soon the Earth, and every lifeform harmonizing with her, will no longer support that perception of reality. **All peoples will join together in a grand moment of awakening.**"

∞ ∞ ∞

"*Universal energy* being released into the Earth's atmosphere is the basic vibration that will sustain and complete mankind's internal transformation.

"Great stellar beings have served your race since it first arrived on Earth. The energies they radiate toward the planet have guided your people through a vast series of vibratory alterations. All civilizations on Earth have experienced their influence, and every human being has been nurtured by their light.

"Earth is now preparing to receive energies focused by these stellar beings which will create a vibratory bridge into realms of light your race has not yet perceived.

"When the transformation sweeping through the Primary Matrix is complete, **five new frequencies of light will be revealed**. These new frequencies will greatly assist in raising the vibratory rate of the human body, so that it may pass through what is termed a Primary Light Threshold. **This will also allow the physical tissues to sustain and transmit the light of Divine**

Presence, thus enabling the physical body to transcend time and space."

The three architects continued:

"The Earth's energy system is being redesigned to interface with the new system of twelve frequencies.[1] As the Primary Matrix adjusts to these frequencies, your people will become aware of the electrical fields surrounding and unifying the entire human race.

"The *Primary Matrix of the Human Race* is also being altered to create new electrical parameters for your race. This matrix manifests one unified electrical pattern which creates the design of the entire human race. The electrical radiation of the Human Primary Matrix is known as the *Collective Mind*.[2]

"The most intense focus of these transformative energies is being centered within the individual human mind, as well as the Collective Mind.

"Light energy flowing through the mind alters the tissues of the brain and, as the brain tissue is altered, so is the entire physical body.

"The mind is simply an instrument of perception utilized by the soul to receive and transmit information. **Only the soul can know. Once humans allow their souls to fully focus and express through their minds, they will have complete mastery**

---

1. The Earth's original seven frequencies plus the five new ones.
2. The collective field of consciousness focused by the entire human race. The Collective Mind permeates and unifies the race, allowing information to be shared by all members. (Most people are not consciously aware of this sharing.)

over the environment and will be able to command the elements to obey their wills. Some on Earth have fully understood the electrical nature of the universe and have mastered the transformation of matter. The wonders created by these individuals have greatly altered mankind's expression on Earth.

"When your people comprehend the totality of light and allow it to illuminate their minds, they will create with thought impulses — in the same manner the Divine Presence creates the universes of light. No era of your planet's history can compare to the magnificence this experience will bring."

∞   ∞   ∞

"The human race is woven into the electrical essence of Earth in a way your people have not understood. Every level of transformation she is undergoing will be experienced by humanity as well.

"The seven realms of Earth all vibrate in harmony with the seven chakra centers and energy fields (auric field) of the human being.

"As the Earth's seventh energy seal begins to vibrate at a new frequency, so will the seventh seal (crown chakra) of the human energy field. The new frequency of the crown chakra will then resonate with the eighth energy field surrounding the physical body. Through this union, currents of energy will be released into the physical tissues from the eighth energy center just above the top of the head.

"Magnetic interfaces within the human mind, which have facilitated the experience of individual consciousness, will then be able to interface directly with Divine Mind. Your people have experienced the world of senses and the multiplicity of physical form; soon they will experience worlds beyond the physical senses, as they realize their unity with all Creation."

∞ ∞ ∞

"Since we three are the focus of Divine Mind that originally designed the human form, we are now being utilized to achieve its present transformation.

"**We are altering the central nervous system of the human body**, restructuring its electrical system to accommodate all *twelve* frequencies of light vibration. This will allow your people to fully experience the transformation that is embracing Earth.

"The incoming stellar energies are now activating light codes stored within the human energy system to vibrate the substance known as DNA. **The DNA will then participate in restructuring the physical body.** This will also increase the central nervous system's ability to respond to the vibratory frequencies we are transmitting."

"The seven frequency levels of their physical nature are one of the greatest mysteries your people have yet to explore. These frequencies are interwoven within the electrical core of the soul, in the same way that the seven realms are interwoven into the Earth's Matrix. They form the body of light — the aura, or human energy field — that adorns the soul.

"Through the expression of these frequencies, the human body exists on seven different levels of purpose and function.

Since these levels have not been consciously experienced by your people, many aspects of the physical body are yet unknown to them.

"As you know, the crown chakra (seventh center) has been the focal point through which the soul receives and transmits divine energy. However, **the alterations now underway will transfer that capacity directly into the nucleus of every cell.**

"Light impulses, vibrating through the transmission point of the DNA, are redesigning each cell to accommodate the Divine Presence without support from surrounding electrical fields. The glands and organs within the physical body are also being redesigned to participate fully in their new electrical reality.

"The entire human body is being elevated in electrical frequency. This will unify all seven levels of the energy field and prepare each cell to accommodate any frequency of light vibration."

I wondered if people would start to glow like these light beings....

"Our transmission is a vitally important bridge of light that has been prepared with great care. The Earth has been directly served by Divine Presence for thousands of years in preparation for this event. Many times Divine Mind has radiated light within the human mind, inspiring your race through one of its own. In countless ways these enlightened individuals have influenced mankind during moments of great change, inspiring an ever-increasing awareness of life.

"So it is with the transmission now being sent to Earth. The inspiration flowing into the Primary Matrix of the Human Race will unite the entirety of mankind. Once humans have experienced the higher realms of light, they will be ready to participate with Earth in the final portion of this transformation."

"Now John, with the aid of everyone gathered here, we will focus through you to contact the Earthman who is recording this information. The twelve frequencies must be balanced within his body, so he can resonate in greater harmony with our energy presence. It is vital that a clear connection be maintained during the completion of our transmission."

A powerful vibration swept me into a vast network of pulsing lights. As energy from the Sanctuary surged through me, I felt an intimate reunion with the essence of Earth.

A highly-focused pulsation of energy vibrated through me into the man on Earth, and I became aware of a radiant design within his physical body. Spirals of blue light were flowing into corresponding points within his body, forming an intense electrical bond between us. . . . It was a fascinating interaction!

∞   ∞   ∞

Then I was back in the Sanctuary with the two violet angels. Golden-amber energy flowed from their forms, and their headbands pulsed in a different manner than before.

As their energy fused with mine, I understood that they would help me experience the five new realms of light being revealed within the Primary Matrix. I knew these realms would influence the Earth in countless ways.

The entire gathering focused a unified thought into my consciousness:

"The final phase of our transmission is underway, and the transformation of Earth is nearly complete.

"You have served your race well. Be at peace."

∞   ∞   ∞

"The decree has been given: 'No longer shall mankind fear death!' You are being asked to help the people of Earth understand that death is only an illusion. They must release their fear of death in order to know the truth of their own immortality."

See page 8

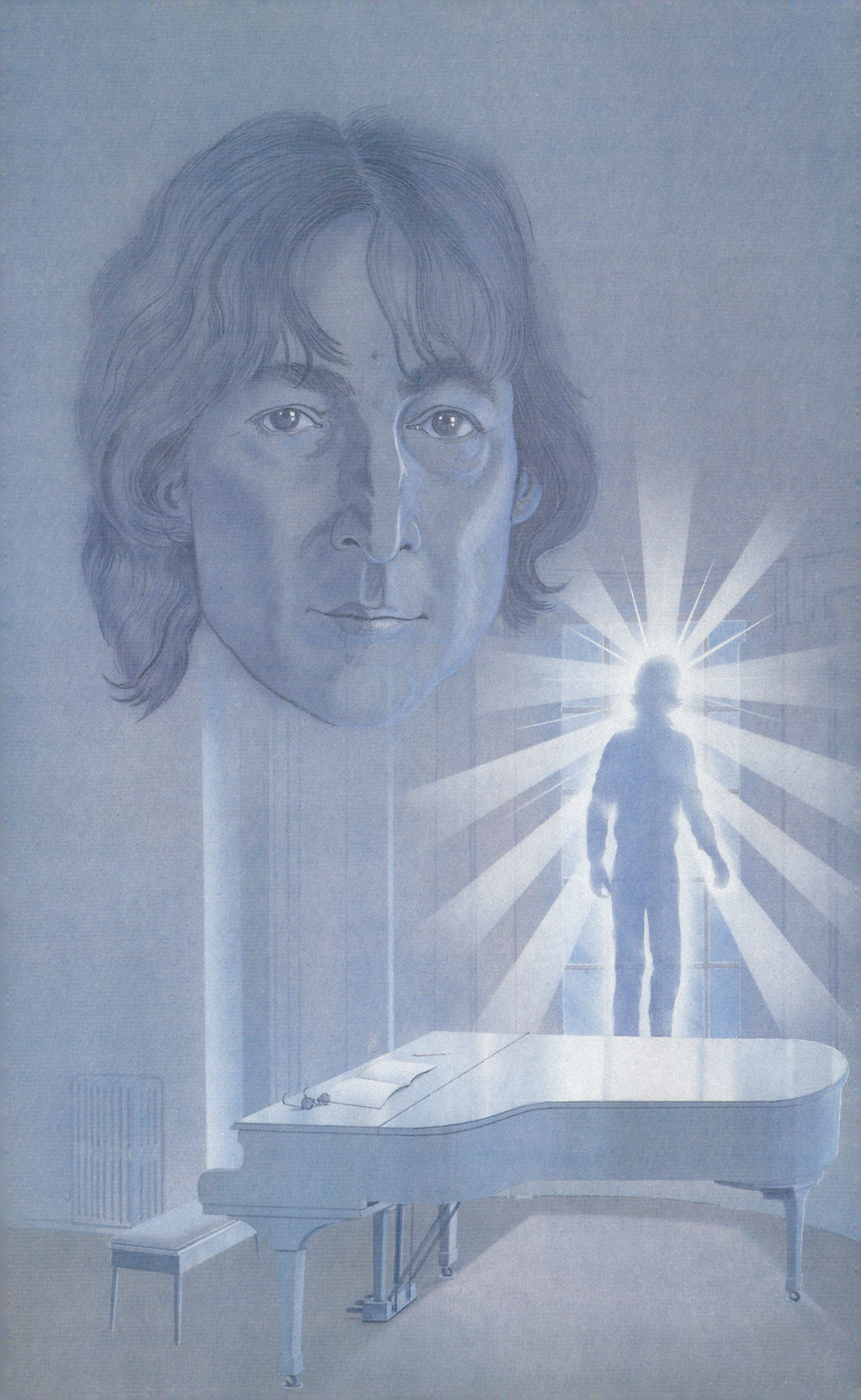

One solitary musical note filled the air. I couldn't say when or where it began... but as I listened, an enormous crystal lotus flower appeared in the glen.

An opening formed in its side. "The time has come, John. This is the Temple of the Octave. This is your beginning."

See page 13

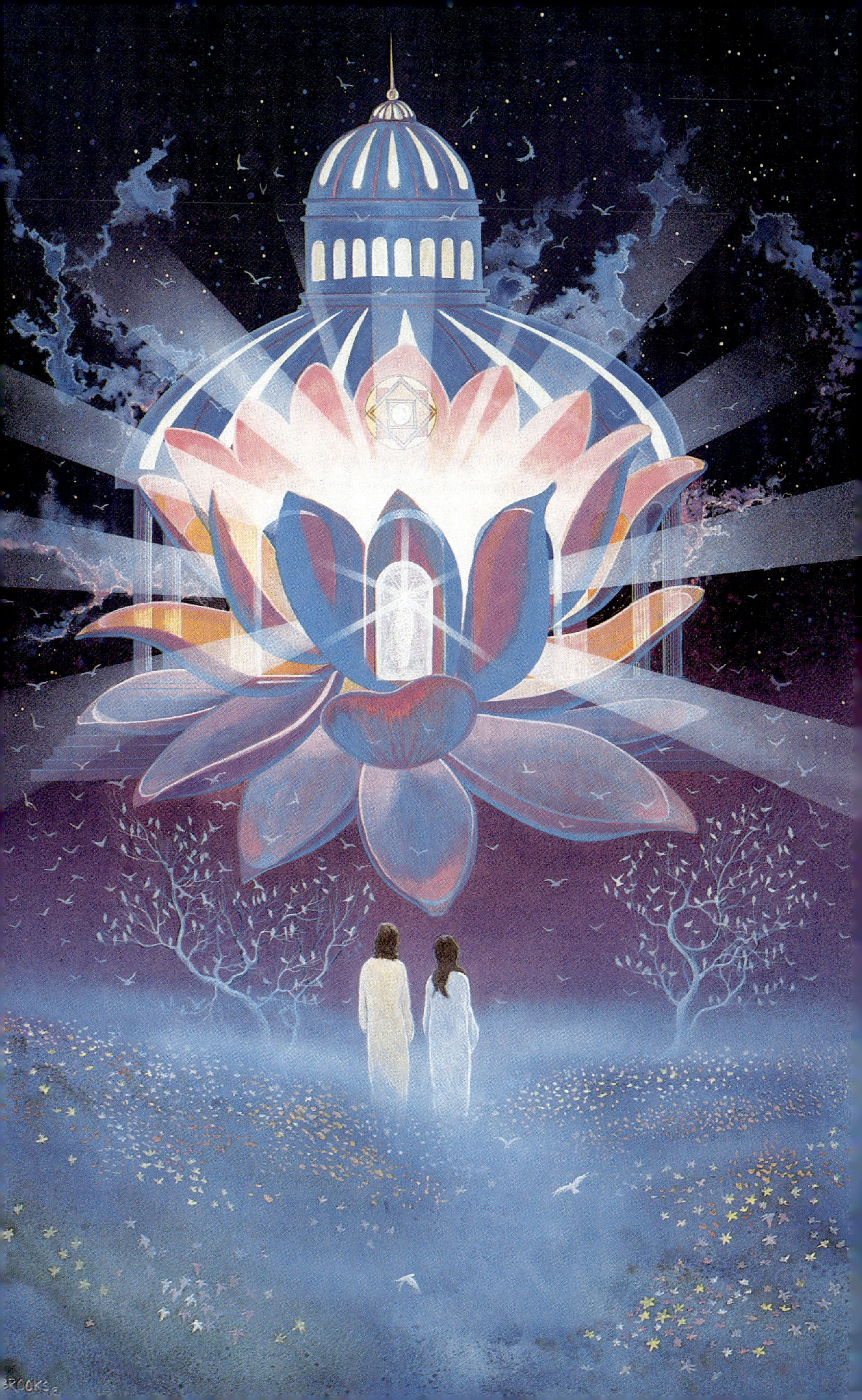

"These three are the Keepers of the Gate." Projecting from their hands were brilliant streams of light, filled with tiny rainbow particles. These beams formed a triangular pyramid far above our heads. As the apex grew more dense, the particles swirled within the pyramid, creating beautiful multicolored designs.

See page 32

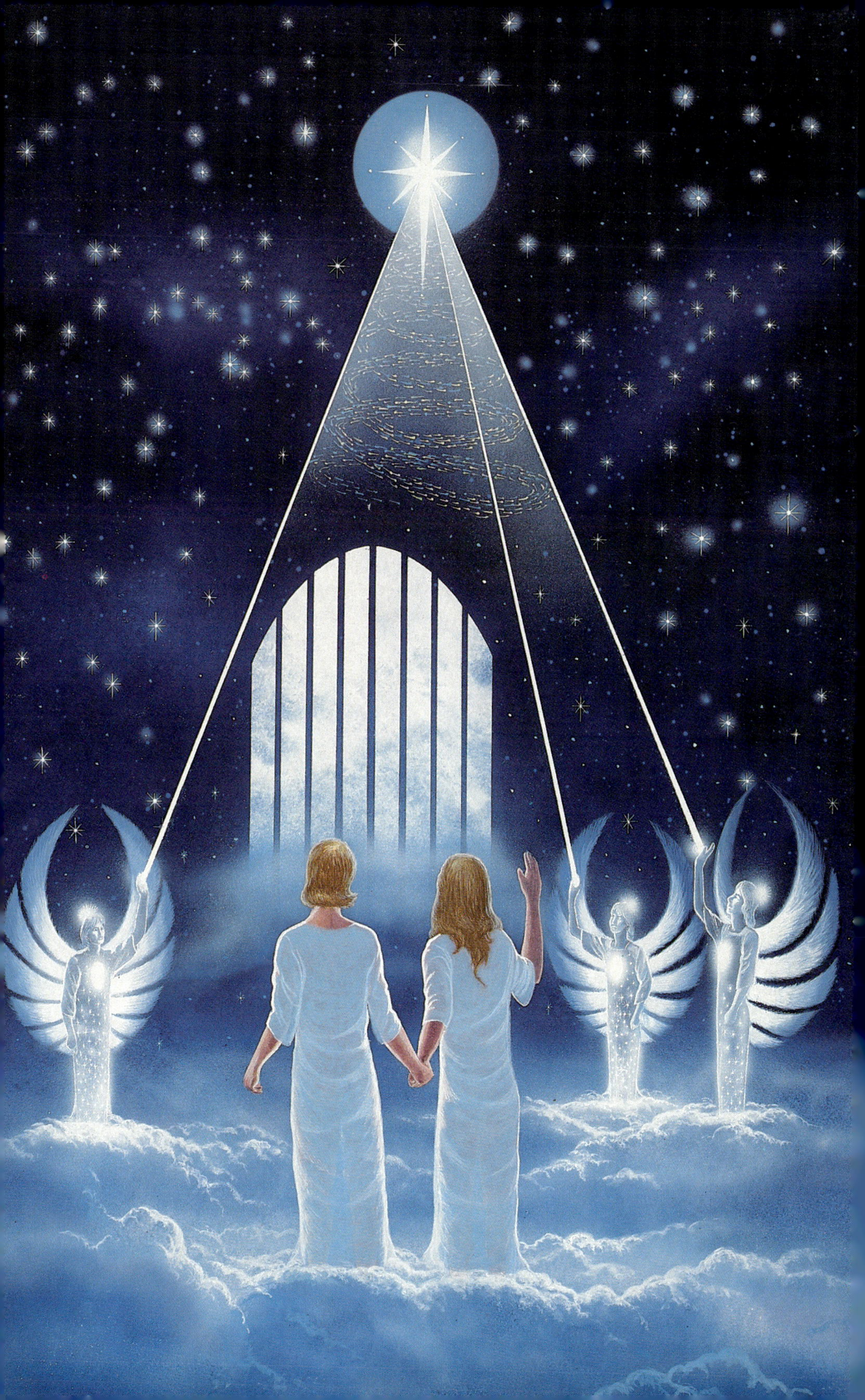

They looked different from the other angels I'd seen. Delicate patterns of violet and purple pulsed from the center of their bodies, flowing out as two majestic wings. Each had a band of gold light around its forehead, and communicated by flashing light pulses from these bands.

See page 61

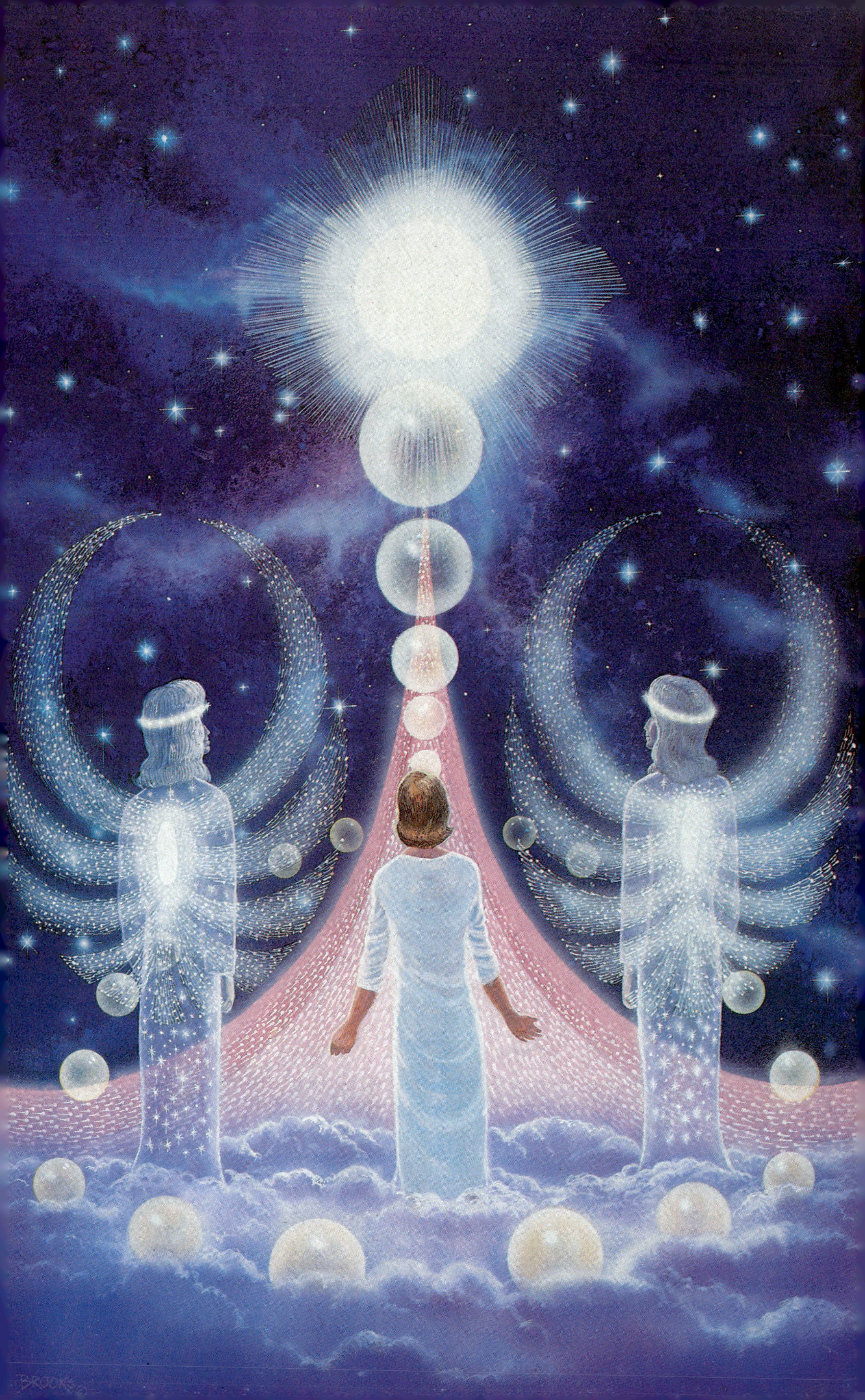
BROOKS

"I am the Living God who walked the Earth clothed in flesh as the one your race calls Jesus.

"I am the Living God who has walked the Earth in every other form as well."

See page 128

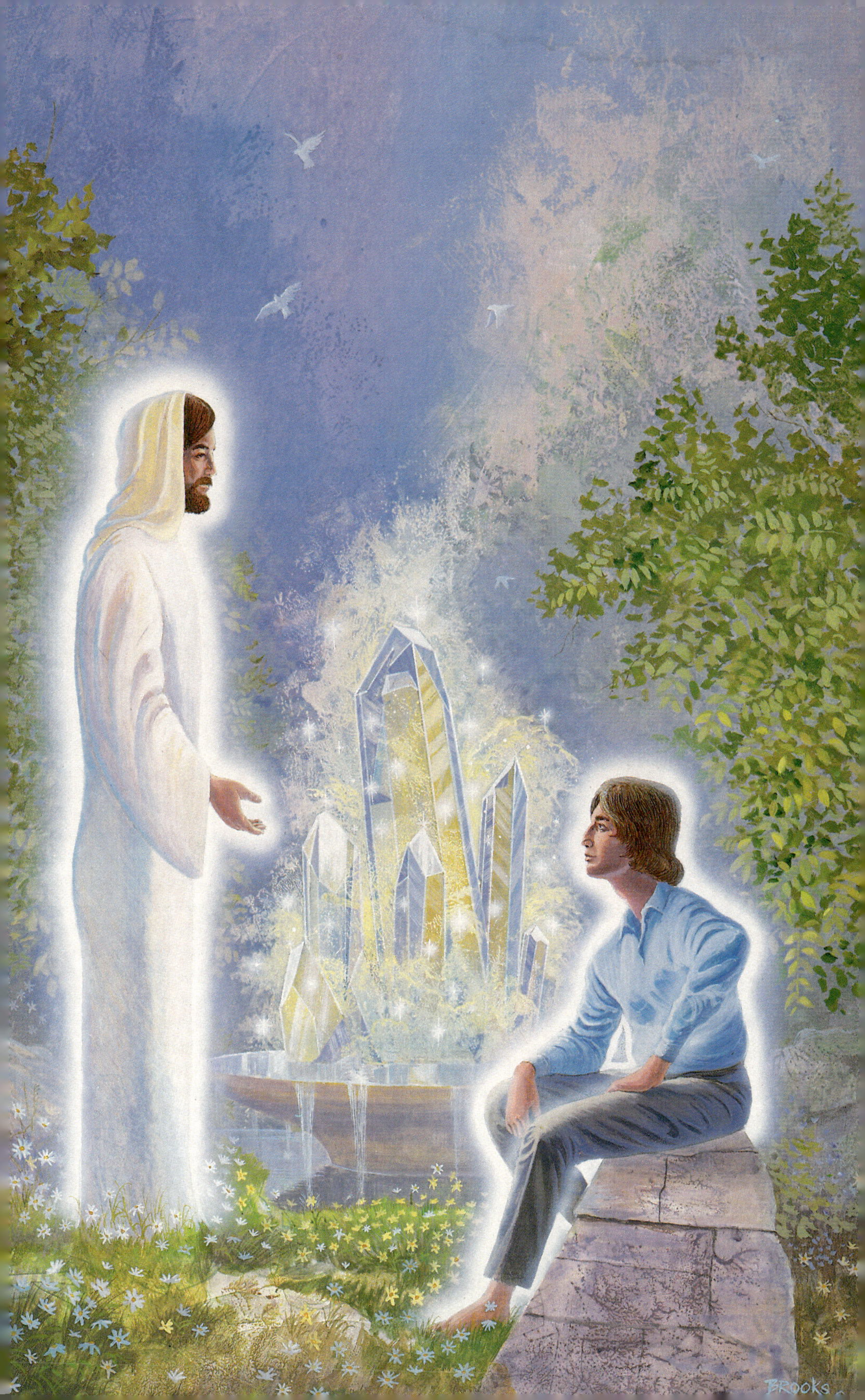
BROOKS

"Alice laughed. 'There is no use trying,' she said. 'One can't believe impossible things.'

"'I daresay you haven't had much practice,' said the Queen. 'When I was your age, I always did it for half an hour a day. Why sometimes I've believed as many as six impossible things before breakfast.'"

LEWIS CARROLL

Seven

ASCENSION: THE DESTINY OF HUMANITY

Activity filled the Sanctuary. My violet friends had summoned a multitude of angels who circled us in an elaborate spiral of color. The spiral first turned golden amber and then the same electric-blue that had flowed through me into the Earth.

The violet angels explained:

"Each of Earth's invisible realms is essential to the final phase of our transmission, and each is represented within this spiral. They hold keys of light that will release treasures long held in the secret regions of Earth. Their keys also complete the link with energy transmissions stellar beings are focusing into the Primary Matrix."

Golden particles from the Sanctuary flowed into the blue spirals rotating around the man on Earth. They bathed his tissues and then streamed out — duplicating on Earth's surface the pattern around his body. A faint violet light pulsed from these entrance points on the planet.

"Our transmission is being adjusted to the highest frequency possible for an earthly vibratory connection," the angels continued.

"Many beings on other worlds wait for the signal to begin tasks which will directly benefit your planet. Using *grid transfer light codes*,[1] we have created a bridge between those worlds and Earth. The node points of Earth's grid system now resonate with those of the other worlds, allowing energy waves to move freely among them. This interaction is necessary for the services those worlds will provide to Earth."

"We are now ready to anchor the five new frequencies. They will be contained within Earth's node points until adjustments to the Earthman's electrical system are complete. Then they will be released into the grid network to merge with the unified electrical patterns of your race and the planet. The grid transfer light codes will open up communication with all twelve frequencies of Earth."

∞   ∞   ∞

The spiral of angels spun even faster around us. Now encased in amber energy, my two violet friends faced each other and began a rapid vibration. Layers of light particles formed around them, fusing into a brilliant diamond skin. Energy

---

1. The interfacing light codes between energy grids of the seven realms of Earth. Their functioning will facilitate communication between Earth's different realms once the new grid system is in place. These codes will also guide Earth's transition into its new dimensional reality and star grouping.

surged through me into the angelic spiral and was reflected back — crystallizing into a golden jewel around us.

A high-frequency tone came from the two angels. Arching their heads back, they projected violet laser beams from their eyes that joined in an apex near the faceted part of the crystal.

Waves of energy moved up through them, streaming out the apex, through the crystal facets and into the angelic spiral. The energy was then transmitted into the Primary Matrix.

Five powerful pulses were transmitted in this manner, each changing the color of energy that blended the spiral together. Although I'd never seen these colors, I somehow understood the alterations each one created in the Matrix. With every pulse my awareness flared out to encompass the planet, as the energy was stored in the node points of Earth's grid system.

Then the violet angels dissolved their laser connection and the transmission ended.

"These currents are now grounded and aligned with the planet, and the transfer sequence is underway. We will return to Earth, where you will directly experience the many levels of her transformation. Your experiences will be shared with the Earthman through the transmission points connecting your essence with his. Great care must be taken to preserve the accuracy of our transmission, since these realities are often difficult to convey in present Earth languages."

"Your people are approaching a mental and verbal fusion point. Their communication methods will completely change once these new frequencies are blended into the human experience.

"Electronically-coded information will soon be released into Earth's grid system to be interwoven with the electrical essence of the human race. Uniquely-designed cranial nerves[2] will be the initial physical link. **These nerves will receive the information codes and focus them into the pituitary gland, where they will be translated for the physical tissues.** Then the entire body will be able to access the informational currents directly, speeding humanity's evolution toward higher levels of awareness and activity."

"Remember, John, the human race chose Earth as their home in an act of conscious alignment with her Primary Matrix. The incoming intelligence fully understood Earth's multilevel nature and deeply appreciated her internal state of preparation.

"At that time an alignment was established with the Matrix which would eventually support communication between humanity and Earth's higher frequencies. The event planned so long ago, although forgotten at the conscious level, is now beginning to take place."

Now I remembered! I had known this in my deepest subconcious link with the Collective Human Mind. No wonder I felt so much joy when I merged with Earth's consciousness.

The two angels continued:

"Humanity's interfacing energy grid is presently being

---

2. Cranial nerves pick up all sensory information, including sight, sound, taste and smell.

redesigned to accept the initial sequences of our transmission. The light code transmission is dissolving the frequencies that have separated and defined the various realms of Earth. Soon all her realms will blend into one unified expression of Divine Mind."

∞ ∞ ∞

"To help humanity more easily understand these activities, we have interfaced with the human race through a higher octave of the man recording our thoughts."

A different energy now flowed from the man's body. When our frequencies blended, I was in direct communication with what could be called his *"higher self."*

"Welcome, John. The complexity of the final transmission sequences requires a conscious connection between you and humanity. I am the resonance bridge that will serve this purpose."

I paused to absorb the impact of our connection.

"The human race is becoming an eighth-level essence," the violet angels added. "This next transmission sequence will assist in refocusing the tri-polarity of the human mind into a single, unified awareness.

"The first of the five new frequencies will blend the seven human energy fields. At the same time, new structural light codes will be transmitted from the planet's higher frequency realms. These new frequencies will stabilize in the physical tissues of Earth and humanity, initiating a vital series of events.

"New sciences and abilities will enable your people to interface their unified awareness directly with the consciousness of Earth and her invisible realms. This unification is essential to the services Earth and her people will provide to the universe."

∞   ∞   ∞

Globes of energy danced around me, creating beautiful designs — like jewels glistening under rippling water. Waves of interweaving color formed condensation points where the energies overlapped. Then a subtle transformation took place — the globes gradually became central radiance points within the forms of delicate, fairylike beings.

As the fairy-forms grew more defined I felt a gentle, loving presence seeking to share my awareness. The violet angels helped refine my focus, and I found myself in direct communion with the Presence of Earth.

I cried out in joy! I knew my Mother Earth again, but in a way I never had before — as an exquisite symphony of sound.

"Etanali, my beloved. *Etanali*. It is a joy to share my thoughts with you in a way you can understand.

"Are you surprised that I have thoughts to share? Just as humans are more than their physical bodies, I am also more than mine.

"Many of your people have heard me speak to them directly, and many more have heard me through one of my beloved thoughtforms.

"Yes, John, these little shining ones are thoughtforms I have created with impulses of energy from my mind. They serve me on every level of my being, performing vital functions within each of my realms.

"The solar and stellar energies that nourish me are shared with your race through the loving participation of these radiant little beings. Many of your people have seen them, but few are aware of their function. Soon the fairies, as you call them, will reveal themselves to your race, and the ancient fountains will again spring forth."

"We are entering the initial phase in a sequence of events that will blend all my realms into a completely unified expression of divine love. Humanity's conscious cooperation with me is essential to achieving our shared destiny.

"Solar energies are awakening dormant abilities within your people, and they will soon be able to interface directly with the living, creative ethers. Then the ancient thoughtforms of sin and separation will be transmuted, my physical being will become purified of all pollution, and your people will experience the pristine beauty of my original form.

"Dynamic energies now crystallizing in my physical structure will create the frequency alignments necessary for my direct communication with humanity again. How my heart yearns to reestablish a conscious, loving communion with all my children."

That stirred up some interesting thoughts.... What a trip it would be to walk on the Earth and talk with her at the same time.

∞   ∞   ∞

My violet friends were in the Sanctuary when I returned.

"We have completed the necessary alignments between the Earth and humanity. We will now escort you to the Solar Presence who cares for Earth, known to your people as their Sun. This magnificent being will initiate you and all of humanity into a new solar reality.

"We have loved and cared for you in every way. We have guided you through many experiences and given you visions of the paradise to come. As you journey on, you will feel our unity and we will share your new discoveries. And as we care for Earth and her peoples, John, your love will be given with our own."

Waves of gold pulsed from the two angels, becoming a luminous peach color, laced with weblike lightning.

The lightning formed into spirals, pulling me into their center with tremendous force. I whirled faster and faster within the flickering web, until the spirals dissolved in a burst of diamond light. I felt frozen in time — I still sensed the intense energy, but could no longer experience it directly.

Slowly I regained my focus within the brilliance. Ripples of light swept through me, as a powerful presence merged with my consciousness. It was the Solar Being.

Instead of the burning gaseous ball I would have expected, I was wrapped in a love so powerful and pure it penetrated space to commune with all the beings in its care.

I witnessed the solar breath anointing Earth, scattering a radiant net of jewels around her. Millions of thoughtforms moved within that breath in a rhythmic exchange between Sun and Earth, Father and Mother, masculine and feminine.

"Welcome, my child. I am the embrace of light that quickens Earth. The radiant thoughtforms you see moving toward Earth are created by my desire to embrace your planet.

"Many of your visionaries have experienced my presence as a celestial being. They have shared my wisdom with Earth and helped complete the bridge of light that now allows her to receive the energy of the stars directly.

"The stellar beings who have communed with me through countless æons are now in direct contact with the human race. Earth's energy pulsations are being altered so these beings can blend their energies in a totally new pattern within her Primary Matrix.

"Thought impulses, of a magnitude your race cannot yet detect, are altering the frequencies of my energy pulsations. My own internal transformation will eventually affect every planet in my care.

"Your people have named this planetary gathering '*solar system*,' but they have comprehended only a fragment of the intricate exchange of energies between the other worlds and their own. The energies directed to Earth by the stellar beings will enable humanity to perceive its true relationship with the other planets."

"The physical body is adjusting to the new focus of the human race. **Energy that has been stored in the tissues will be released through the entire body, altering the interaction of**

many existing organs and activating newly-created energy exchange centers. These centers will interface with Earth's higher frequency realms through the *solar center of the human heart*.[3]

"A light blending in the human heart will harmonize its solar center with new solar substances. These substances are being transmitted from Earth's higher frequency realms, where they have been balanced and adjusted for human assimilation. This change will facilitate an equally important transformation in the atomic structure of the blood.

"Blood serves in many ways, one of which is the purification of the body's emotional centers. These centers are designed to receive and transmit energy waves that carry the substance of every human emotion.

"The wave patterns of certain emotions interlock in the tissues around the emotional centers, causing destructive energy blockages. Blood flowing through these tissues transmits a very-high-frequency light pulse that helps release the blockages.

"**Soon the human electrical system will interface with that of Earth in a very different way, and it will be impossible for these blockages to form**. Then the blood will serve the body in a higher capacity — absorbing high-frequency energies and making them accessible to the tissues. This will assist each cell in directly receiving and transmitting the divine energy flow."

---

3. A physical location in the human heart where light pulses from the Sun trigger energy releases throughout the body. This energy is utilized by the blood in healing and revitalizing the body.

"The Divine Presence is *everywhere* at once, expressing in a vast number of ways to create the many realms of existence.

"Soon you will behold the Creator directly, for you are destined to help your people express qualities of Divine Presence very few of them have ever experienced. But first your vibratory rate must be increased. Celestial beings have come to prepare you for this communion.

"I am the expression of divine love that quickens the Earth."

These words surged through me in a burst of diamond energy. As my awareness dissolved into the brilliance, I *became* the light.

∞   ∞   ∞

Suddenly the air filled with exquisite music. I was able to briefly experience the totality of Earth and the magnitude of the transformation underway. Then I was back in the presence of the Solar Being.

"I embrace you, my child, as we share the end of our communion. A great Stellar Being who has served your people through countless æons waits to anoint them more directly. But before you experience this blessing there is additional information I would have you reveal to your people.

"Earth's present transformation is interwoven in a divine plan that encompasses the whole of Creation. Focused activity over millions of years has prepared Earth for this event. Many seemingly-unrelated contributions, including the music you created while living on Earth, have supported this moment.

"Soon the emotional body will be able to transmit higher-frequency light codes, enabling solar radiance to be expressed directly through the physical tissues. Some of the music created on Earth in recent times has supported this ability, and will be brought into an even clearer focus in the near future.

"You will be involved in a new expression of music on the Earth plane. However, to fully experience its benefits, your people must first realize their own multidimensional nature.

"Divine radiance is beginning to illuminate the entire planet, and a moment is approaching when every race of every realm will express this truth: Within the light, we are One."

∞   ∞   ∞

"Eternal harmony is the harmony of consciousness... all things live and move in it; yet it remains remote, undisturbed and peaceful. This is the God of the believer, and the God of the knower. All vibrations, from the finest to the grossest, are held together by this harmony... both creation and destruction take place in order to uphold it. Its power ultimately attracts each being toward the everlasting peace."

HAZRAT INAYAT KHAN

Eight

HEAVEN: THE KINGDOM ETERNAL

Waves of brilliant light pulsed from the Solar Being and I was able to experience the celestial entities gathering near the Sun.

I couldn't totally connect with their light essence, but the magnitude of the energy I did experience was almost overwhelming. I was trying to communicate with them when the Solar Being projected these thoughts:

"Cease your effort, my child. These entities are sealed in an envelope of energy vibrating at a rate beyond your awareness. Their true presence cannot be expressed within my frequencies.

"They anchor their essence within my essence, clothing themselves with my light substance in order to serve the Earth. Soon you will be able to appreciate their full beauty, as they escort you into higher realms of light.

"At this time their main function is to align and adjust energy currents transmitted by the *Primary Solar Being*[1] near the

---

[1]. Located near the center of the Milky Way Galaxy, this entity is responsible for focusing energy substance to all suns throughout our galaxy.

center of this galaxy. This activity serves a dual purpose: to stimulate envelopes of solar energy surrounding Earth, and to illuminate the solar center within the human heart.

"**Alterations within the heart solar center are among the most important changes being experienced by your race**. The solar essence that has been expressed primarily through the mind will now be expressed through the heart, greatly expanding the capacity to love.

"When this occurs, your people will be uplifted into a new level of awareness — enfolded by the peace that passes all understanding. This realization is a *solar initiation.* It will create the foundation for the global event your people have always dreamed of — **the experience of Heaven on Earth.**

"As the solar radiance intensifies within the human heart and begins to flow into Earth's atmosphere, a great calming will be experienced throughout your world. The discord that has created such great suffering will be transmuted into total harmony and love. Then your people will directly experience the full magnitude of their healing abilities.

"**Love is the creative force that designed and sustains the universe. When your people truly understand this, they will be able to instantly fulfill all their earthly needs — using the same energy that created the stars.**"

"It is time to continue your journey into the ever-increasing brilliance of the stellar realms. I am in direct communion with the radiant being who awaits you. I have adjusted the connecting energy grid to accommodate your energy pattern and light frequency. Bless you, my child."

∞ ∞ ∞

The Solar Being began to pulse, transmitting a series of rainbow patterns into space. I was immediately aware of the celestial beings who were anointing Earth. They surrounded me with a beautiful blue light, and for an instant I experienced something of their true nature. Gathering around the Solar Being, they shared the essence of their light transmission to Earth through a brilliant series of energy pulsations.

Then they closed around me again, and we began flying at a fantastic speed through the grid patterns projected into space. Soaring freely through these patterns, I experienced indescribable changes in my awareness.

The journey ended in a burst of scarlet light, and I was in the presence of a magnificent Stellar Being.

An amazing flow of light pulsed from the Being — so intense that I couldn't focus at first. With total concentration I was finally able to receive the energy flow.

"I welcome you with the love of our joyous Creator.

"I clothe your essence with my luminous breath and sustain you with my vitality in service of your divine activity.

"My light is revealed to you that you may continue to experience the realms of Creation beyond my inner gate.

"I reveal my light to the Earthman, that he may share our communion and record for humanity your experience within these realms.

"The destiny of Earth is unique among the worlds I have communed with. She is being redesigned with a multidimensional Primary Matrix that will enable her to shift her energy frequencies and experience other dimensions of Creation.

"The celestial beings who accompanied you here are directly involved in the alteration of Earth's dimensional structure. Their assistance is required because the quality of light necessary to blend the dimensional frequencies of the Matrix is beyond my ability to transmit.

"These beings designed the *universal coordinate pattern*[2] that will guide the planet as the dimensional shifts occur. They also delivered the first series of sequential phasing patterns, the transition codes.

"Now I will focus my light upon Earth to align her existing energy grid network with the new patterns. These alignments will stimulate new energy centers on Earth's surface and will reactivate many of her *ancient centers*. Energy will be imprinted directly from the universal currents into specific centers, in both singular and *sequential light codes*, to create an interface with the Primary Matrix.

"This will also allow your people to absorb any portion of the energy imprint. Once they experience the transformations initiated by these currents, they will become aware of my multi-dimensional reality — and their own as well.

"Only then will the beings who bring the greatest changes enter my gate; for, once they do so, all thoughtforms that no

---

2. The grid design or pattern within the universal grid system of the galaxy that establishes the placement of stars and other heavenly bodies. Similar to a stellar map.

longer resonate with the new Primary Matrix will be dissolved. Then Earth and the human race will complete their transformation very quickly.

"Once these transformations are complete, humanity will be responsible for re-establishing the planet's harmonic balance. While creating this balance, your people will demonstrate abilities that will surpass anything they have previously experienced.

"The harmony resulting from the transformation, combined with the peace being expressed by the heart solar center, will create a perfect blend of supportive energies. Earth will be nourished by these energies while final preparations are being made for the dimensional shift."

"A veil of energy was placed around the planet in response to needs expressed by the human race when it first arrived on Earth. The Solar Being will soon direct the radiant ones surrounding Earth to dissolve this veil. Then Earth will be nourished directly by my energy, and humanity will recognize the intelligence and vitality of the universe.

"The Solar Being is now radiating light frequencies that are redesigning the energy interface between your race and the stellar realms, to allow for direct communication between them. This will initiate a metamorphosis within the Collective Human Mind that will enable the Soul's level of intelligence to focus with much greater clarity in the conscious awareness of your race.

"**Earth is about to begin a journey through the universe**

unlike any experience she has ever known. I have nurtured and cared for this planetary entity from the beginning, and I will continue to do so throughout time.

"The celestial beings who brought you here have returned to guide you to the center of the universe. Bless you, my child."

∞   ∞   ∞

In a great flash of golden light, the frequency gate within the Stellar Being opened. My guides surrounded me again, and we passed through the threshold. We flew through layers of diamond and bright-blue light, each layer containing a frequency gate similar to the one within the Stellar Being.

Each time we passed through a stargate, my celestial guides became more luminous. Finally they blended together in a brilliant rose-gold light, and our speed immediately decreased.

Waves of radiant beings greeted us by exchanging cobalt light pulsations with my circle of guides. Forming an intricate blue and gold design, these beings enclosed us within their glowing presence.

Then, vibrating rapidly, they filled the interior of the design with music that was entirely new to me. Each note blossomed into thousands of harmonic variations, creating a complex symphony of *living* sound. It was an amazing production!

As I listened, I understood the deeper meaning of their symphony and why these beings had gathered around us. They were thoughtform creations, sent as the vanguard of the Galactic Being. I knew I would experience his presence directly, once the galactic energy was focused by the man recording my transmission.

When the man's awareness had expanded enough, a surge of energy created a glow within my circle of guides. As the glow intensified, the symphony ended and a brilliant cascade of energy poured through me.

The beings pulsed an iridescent diamond energy into our circle, illuminating the design around us. My guides briefly absorbed the energy, then transferred it into my awareness. I was filled with the presence of the Galactic Being.

"I embrace you, my child, as I embrace Earth and every expression of divine light upon and within her wondrous being.

"My existence is recorded in the ancient memory of your race as the Eastern Gate of Creation. I am now activating that memory by transmitting new light frequencies through the Solar Being who cares for Earth.

"I am preparing your people to inherit the radiant kingdoms of the New Earth, for that beautiful entity was conceived specifically for them.

"When my light codes are transmitted into the fabric of Earth, humanity will be able to directly receive the full magnitude of divine light. **The human race has the ability to wield the divine light, just as I do. Soon they will remember this ability and be able to fashion material substance from the pure energy of that light**.

"For æons I have prepared Earth to receive the expression of divine love that will soon be focused through mankind. It is vitally important that your people consciously understand the exact nature of this preparation.

"In response to the new light codes, the Primary Matrix of the Human Race is being reblended with Earth's Matrix. A vast assortment of divinely-engineered 'tools' stands ready to assist in these alterations, waiting only for humanity to become aware of their purpose and location.

"As I transmit the final codes, I will also transfer the focus of divine light from within my being into the Soul of the human race. **When your people hold the focus of divine light, they will experience the complete presence of divine nature as an internal reality.** All peoples will experience a simultaneous wave of ecstatic bliss, and the energy flowing through their unified awareness will transmute any last vestiges of fear into pure love. Once this happens, I will be able to transmit the final sequence of dimensional transition codes into the Primary Matrix.

"Then the *estate* they have called Heaven will fully embrace the Earth. It *is* the destiny of the human race to express the brilliance of our Creator's light throughout realms of Creation even I have never experienced.

"Now, my child, prepare to pass through the dimensional threshold of my being. Our beloved Creator awaits you. You have served your people well by sharing this journey with them. Know that Earth will always remember you as a man of peace."

∞ ∞ ∞

They will soon *consciously* re-experience my family of light and share what they have learned with others of their kind."

"Now, as the Earth has called you, I shall call you: John. Rise and drink of this living water."

I stood beside the crystal fountain and knelt to taste the water. Then, as we embraced, I was consumed with the greatest joy I have ever known.

Once again, I was totally united with the Lord of Creation.

∞   ∞   ∞

Within the clarity of that union, I knew everything I had been shown would come to pass — for it is indeed a reality within the Mind of God.

Following these experiences, I have focused primarily on assisting humanity and the Earth to raise their vibratory rates in preparaton for the dimensional shift. Many of us are involved in various aspects of this same focus.

Having divine awareness while in a physical body is the ultimate experience in the "outer dimensions" of Creation. When the shift occurs, it is my desire to experience this "new dispensation" in a human form. I expect to be with you as we reap the harvest from humanity's long journey of discovery.

I love you all,

John

Fountain of Light

I've lived as a king on Earth,
Seen the palaces in the sky.
How few of us know its worth
'Til the moment when we die.

For then the illusions fade away,
And our eyes can finally see
The radiant worlds of Heaven
That await both you and me.

And we'll bathe in a crystal fountain,
A fountain filled with holy light.
And within this crystal fountain
All our pains shall soon take flight.

All our deeds will be forgiven,
All our wounds be healed aright,
And we'll behold the wonders of Heaven
As we bathe in the Fountain of Light.

Now I live as a being in Heaven,
I dwell in the palaces on high.
Yet I still call out to the Earth,
I merely passed on—I did not die.

All my illusions—they are gone,
And my eyes can finally see
The radiant light of Heaven,
That bathes both you and me.

For I've bathed in the crystal fountain,
A fountain filled with holy light.
And within this crystal fountain
All my pain has taken flight.

All my deeds have been forgiven,
All my wounds been healed aright.
And I've received the Gifts of Heaven
As I bathed in the Fountain of Light.

And I beheld the Lord of Creation
As I was remade in the Fountain of Light.

The Interview

Compiled by Jason Leen in January 1982 from notes taken during conversations with John Lennon.

JASON: Well, John, where would you like to begin?
JOHN: I suppose we should start at the beginning.
JASON: Would that be the moment of your death?
JOHN: No, the beginning for me was a few days earlier, when I began feeling a strong sense of change in the air.
JASON: Were you sensing your death?
JOHN: Not during the week before it actually happened. But I had "seen" my death on several other occasions. Many elements of those premonitions carried through into the night I was shot. It's amazing how those connections are formed.

But this sense of change I'm talking about wasn't connected to any thought of death. It was just a feeling that continued to grow inside me.

On the evening of December 8th, Yoko and I were working at the studio in New York City. I was very involved in my work and happy with what I was doing, but there was still an undercurrent of something out of place. My mind kept drifting back to Sean.

We'd planned to go somewhere to eat with the others, but I decided to call it a day. I just wanted to be at home with Yoko and Sean. You know the rest of that story...

JASON: From the time you entered the tunnel of light, you received almost constant protection and assistance from etheric and angelic sources. Do you know why?

JOHN: Everyone who "dies" is cared for in a very loving, supportive way. I found out later that the particular energy surrounding me at that time protected me from being immersed in a prolonged period of grief over being separated from my family. That's not to say I didn't experience those emotions, just that I wasn't consumed by them. Even then I was being prepared for this work. I couldn't be a spokesman for eternal life and the etheric realms if I was locked into the lower vibrations of grief and pain.

JASON: Is that the primary reason for your return, and for our work together?

JOHN: Yes, with the exception of a few private matters between me and Yoko. I am communicating with humanity to share the reality of life after death with all who will listen. People severely limit their own growth by refusing to acknowledge the existence of the nonphysical realms. The demons some people believe inhabit the spirit worlds are nothing more than creations of their own fragmented fantasies. There's nothing here to be afraid of.

JASON: Have you contacted Yoko since your death?

JOHN: Not in the way you and I communicate, but yes, I've come through to her many times. She has felt my presence, but we've had no solid communication as yet. I think we'll be able to share our thoughts as time passes and we learn to link our present states of being.

JASON: What about Sean and Julian? Have you contacted them?

JOHN: Not on the level I've attempted with Yoko. I haven't wanted to startle them in any way. Perhaps as they grow older we'll be able to communicate in some way, but at the present I visit them only in their dreams. I want to remain as close to them as I can.

JASON: Have you contacted anyone else?

JOHN: Yes, several people who were close to me in my physical life. Most of them felt my presence, but there was no verbal communication. I did what I could to let them know I was near, and we shared a few moments together. That was all.

JASON: What kinds of structures have you seen in your new environment?

JOHN: I've seen and been inside several etheric buildings. Most of them are used for balancing the etheric bodies of people who have recently arrived — healing them, you might say, although that term could seem a bit strange when talking about someone who is no longer "living."

The key here is that there are other regions of existence beyond the physical. People are still alive after they leave the Earth; they just don't have physical bodies.

JASON: Are you influenced in any way by people's thoughts and feelings about you?

JOHN: In the beginning, while my etheric form was unstable, the magnetic pull from people on Earth who wanted me back was almost unbearable at times. But as my balance stabilized and came into clearer focus, I became insulated from those vibrations.

That doesn't diminish my connection with Earth. I continue to relate to humanity in many ways — one of them being my work with you.

JASON: How do you feel about relating back to Earth?

JOHN: I'm in contact with Earth because of my love for the people. It gives me a lot of joy to be able to communicate my feelings and thoughts so clearly.

JASON: What do you see for the future of music?

JOHN: There is little change in store for the next few years ('82 to '85), but I do see variations coming that will bring more spiritual influences into music. The human spirit is unfolding in many ways, and I think people will begin to seek out music that supports their unfoldment. They will be looking to music for inspiration and attunement, rather than just entertainment. This was beginning to happen even before my death.

JASON: Will you be relating musically to Earth again?

JOHN: Yes. I'm still a musician, and that's how I best relate my thoughts and feelings. The music I have to give is sent from my heart — to help raise the vibrations on Earth. I want to help restore everyone's faith in life.

In the etheric realms, music surrounds me constantly, reminding me of its infinite possibilities. It is the supreme method of communication. God communicates with all of Creation through the music of the spheres.

Music is the main connection I have with Earth, and as that connection continues, much of it will be through music.

JASON: What will be the range of your musical communication with Earth?

JOHN: I plan to introduce a couple of albums that relate to my experiences here and the messages I have for the people. Then I plan to bring through an unusual musical collection that will assist people in releasing their physical bodies at the moment of death. It will also enable them to maintain their connection with loved ones on Earth. This will consist of 63 hours of recorded music for the entire family to share with the person who is departing, plus 39 hours of music recorded especially for the person who is passing.

Beyond that I can't say exactly, but my communications to Earth will always be based on the needs of the people there.

JASON: Are you saying that this connection is to be permanent?

JOHN: No. There are many unsettling experiences in store for humanity, and I will remain here long enough to do what I can. Once the balance is achieved and I complete the work that is needed, I'll move on to other adventures.

JASON: Then you can see into our physical future?

JOHN: Yes. Time is a very misunderstood feature of the universe. I can see into the flow of things in a way that allows me an overview of what to you is the future. This is one of the "extras" of the etheric realms, one that some people develop while still alive. It has to do with certain particles of matter moving faster than what you call the speed of light. Some scientists have already discovered this. Once it is fully understood, all forms of interdimensional communication will be possible.

JASON: How do future events you have seen relate to the predictions of others, such as Edgar Cayce?

JOHN: Prior to my death, Yoko and I were quite interested in Cayce's predictions. Much of what he predicted regarding earth changes could eventually happen. I don't want to start any form of panic, but I do believe everyone should be made aware of the possibilities.

JASON: Would you suggest we prepare in some way?

JOHN: People should become aware of what to do in an emergency, that's all. I'm sure a few moments of calm thought will bring several ideas to mind. Above all else, perseverance will be your best ally.

JASON: How do you feel about Yoko right now?

JOHN: I still get very emotional when I think of Yoko, so I won't say much at this time. What I will say is this: I love you, Yoko. You are always in my heart, and someday we will continue our journey through the universe together.

JASON: How do you want people to remember you?

JOHN: Remember me smiling, enjoying life — because no matter what, I surely did that. Remember my words, "Give peace a chance." Don't see me lying in a pool of blood; it was bad enough to be there for a moment—don't keep me there forever. Remember me at a happier time and I'll be content with that.

 I love you. May your lives be filled with love. Above all else, may peace be yours.

∞ ∞ ∞

Ethereal Kiss

Spread your wings
I know you can.
For you're an angel
As well as a woman.

Open your heart,
I know you will.
Though I can't hold you,
I love you still.

Oh Yoko, so many things I left unsaid,
They echo now inside my head.
How I long for your love,
Though I'm nectar fed.
Yes, life goes on,
There's light ahead.

Oh, how can I explain?
Your tears—they fall like rain.
But I'm right here beside you,
Right here beside you.
You know I'll never leave
And go away.

The love we shared
I'd never felt.
The bonds we formed
Death cannot melt.
The rest is very hard
For me to say.

But I share your sorrow,
Hear your cries in the night.
When you're alone in the darkness,
I bring you my light.

I bring you my light,
I share of my bliss.
I adorn your lips
With an ethereal kiss.

Glossary

Akashic Record. Also called the **Akasha, Mind of God,** or **Book of Life.** All data from every level of activity in the manifest realms is electronically encoded into the Akasha. The Akasha is magnetic in nature and capable of detecting and recording electrical activity even at subatomic levels.

Ancient Centers. Specifically-placed geographic centers, each having an unusual energy potential similar to an electrical circuit. Examples include the Great Pyramid of Giza and Stonehenge in England. Due to fluctuations of the Earth's electrical field, these centers are not presently functioning at their original energy levels. In conjunction with the planetary transformation now underway, the electromagnetic activity of these centers is being reactivated.

Ancient Fountains. Natural springs within the Earth that flowed in the past, many of which were thought to have special energies conducive to healing. The Delphic Spring in southern Greece is one example.

Aura. Seven multilayered envelopes of highly-refined energies blended together in an oval pattern around the physical body. The aura is in constant interaction with the environment and with other lifeforms. Once the five new frequencies have been incorporated into our reality, the aura will include twelve of these energy envelopes.

Being. Any entity or personage, as human being, divine being, angelic being, light being, etc. When used without a modifying term in this book, being refers to any entity whose origin was unknown to John.

Bridge. A connection between two energy systems or realms of existence which have differing frequencies. Bridges allow exchange of energy in an exceptionally peaceful and harmonious balance.

Collective Human Mind. Also called the **Racial Mind.** The field of consciousness focused by the entire human race. The Collective Mind permeates and unifies the race, allowing information to be shared by all members. (Most people are not consciously aware of this sharing.)

Collective Human Soul or **Human Soul** or **Soul.** The spark of divine energy that bonds the entire human race together as a single entity. Any changes or transformations that will manifest within the physical body are first brought into alignment within the Soul.

Chakras. Energy centers within the physical body which alter and adjust incoming universal energy to a level the physical body can use as nourishment. The chakras deliver stepped-down energy to the endocrine glands, which then distribute it to the other physical tissues.

Dimensional Frequency Interlocking Patterns. The patterns of energy which join the separate dimensions of space and time into a collective whole.

DNA. Deoxyribonucleic Acid. The DNA is the basic building block of the physical body. It holds the body's electrical blueprint and determines the genetic structure of the cells. The DNA is to be the new distribution center for solar energy, presently distributed through the crown chakra (pituitary gland).

Etanali. Universal greeting which means "I honor the Eternal Presence within you." Similar to "Namaste."

Energy Grid System of Earth. Lines of energy held in specific patterns of radiation established by the Primary Matrix. This system takes in universal energy and steps it down for use by the Matrix. It attracts atoms and holds them in orderly patterns, then steps down their frequency levels and passes them into the Earth's node points for conversion into physical matter.

Eternal Flame of Creation. A permanent manifestation of divine light which is connected with every atom of matter in the physical worlds.

Etheric. Having to do with non-physical reality, where matter and spirit converge at a higher, more refined level.

Ethers. The nonphysical regions of the universe which are commonly perceived to be empty space. Vibrating at a much higher frequency than physical matter, those areas are actually very much alive — filled with information and nourishment for all lifeforms. The ethers serve as a conveyance medium for universal energy.

Five New Frequencies. As the Primary Light Code is extended, five new individual light frequencies will be visible to the human race, creating a system of twelve from the present system of seven. Once these frequencies are grounded, a wider range of emotional expression will also be available on Earth. See Five New Realms of Light.

Five New Realms of Light. Five realms of conscious activity not previously perceivable by humanity, which are related to the five new frequencies. Each realm of light vibrates at a specific frequency and transmits its own color and musical tone. The realms of light exist around the Earth much like the layers of an onion. See Seven Realms of Earth.

Frequency Levels. Vibratory rates, as in cycles-per-second for sound or waves-per-inch for light on the Earth level. Among the frequency levels normally understood on Earth are those pertaining to radio or television, where different stations or channels are broadcast and received at discrete frequencies.

The planet Earth accommodates many individual frequency levels, allowing a great variety of life in many different forms to coexist harmoniously. Each lifeform has a unique frequency range within which it maintains its physical activity. For example, humans do not perceive sound at the frequencies perceived by dogs, dolphins, whales, etc.

We are presently unable to perceive lifeforms operating outside our "normal" frequency range, such as fairies, angels, and other etheric beings. Humans do, however, have the inherent ability to perceive all frequencies — and many people are utilizing that ability in varying degrees.

Grid Transfer Light Codes. The interfacing light codes between energy grids of the seven realms of Earth. Their functioning will facilitate communication between Earth's different realms as the new grid system comes into place. These codes will also guide Earth's transition into its new dimensional reality and star grouping.

Hall of Judgement. See Judgement Day.

"Heavens shall no longer be distant." Human perceptive abilities and the energy envelopes surrounding Earth will be adjusted simultaneously. This will reveal that many celestial bodies are actually closer to the Earth than they previously appeared to be.

Higher Self. A perceived aspect of human consciousness that functions at a higher level of awareness and activity than "normal waking" consciousness. Also known as superconsciousness, this aspect of every human being allows a "knowingness" beyond the "normal" awareness of the conscious mind.

Human Mind. (Uncapitalized) The field of consciousness focused by an individual. The human mind permeates the entire physical form, as well as the etheric bodies.

Human Mind. (Capitalized) See Collective Human Mind.

Human Soul or **Soul.** (Uncapitalized) The divine spark within each of us that is an eternal aspect of God. The human soul is invested with free will, a quality that makes it different from many other types of souls.

Human Soul. (Capitalized) See Collective Human Soul.

Interface. The common boundary between adjacent objects or areas. A shared frequency through which species or realms of differing frequencies may communicate.

Judgement Day. Also **Hall of Judgement**. The experience of recording and self-evaluation occurring at the completion of a life in physical form. During this process the life's activities are recorded in the Akashic Record. The entity also evaluates the life's activities according to goals or objectives established before birth. Any judging is done only by the individual involved.

Light Codes. Coded information transmitted as pure light.

Living Water. The flowing presence of God's Love — the "Life-Giver."

Manifest Realms or **Manifest Worlds.** Worlds composed of three-dimensional matter, such as Earth. Contrasted with etheric realms, where three-dimensional matter cannot exist.

New Codes of Sequential Phasing. New timing patterns transmitted to the Earth and the lifeforms manifested here in preparation for the planetary shift. These codes are altering the fluctuation rate of every atom as it moves continuously between the states of light and matter. This will greatly increase the body's vibratory rate, allowing the tissues to draw in and utilize higher levels of universal energy. See Sequential Light Codes.

New Star Grouping or **New Stellar Grouping.** As Earth shifts to new dimensional levels, a 40-mile-thick energy band or corona of light will be placed around the planet. Different constellations will then be visible in the celestial spectrum and we will see stars which are vibrating beyond the level of our present Primary Light Threshold.

Node Points. Specific points in Earth's Energy Grid System which receive, store, and distribute energy from higher frequencies.

Planetary Phase Shift Sequence. The sequence of vibratory adjustments which will create the extension of the Primary Light Code.

Primary Light Code. The visual spectrum established when a seventh-level race first becomes aligned with a planet. For example, the primary light code of Earth is made up of the seven colors of the rainbow.

Primary Light Threshold. A built-in vibratory resistance in the optic nerve which prevents the passage of frequencies above those of the Primary Light Code. Presently, the "normal" optic nerve can perceive only the frequencies of the Primary

Light Code. The Primary Light Threshold is being altered by the introduction of the five new frequencies of light.

Primary Matrix or **The Matrix.** The core electromagnetic pattern which establishes the basic conditions of the physical planet Earth (including structure, design, shape, size, rate of spin, density, etc.). The Matrix, which is the basic electrical reality of the planet, establishes the primary chord of resonance with which all earthly lifeforms resonate.

Primary Matrix of the Human Race. The central electromagnetic pattern which establishes the structure and design of both the individual human body and mind, and the Collective Human Mind. This matrix envelops and unifies all members of the human race.

Primary Solar Being. Located near the center of the Milky Way Galaxy, this entity is responsible for focusing energy substance to all suns throughout our galaxy.

Reality Sequence of the Human Race. An internal sequence of events encoded in the Human Soul that establishes the nature of the physical transformations the human race will undergo.

Realms of Earth or **Seven Realms of Earth.** Seven frequency levels of activity connected with the Primary Matrix. Each is populated by specific types of beings. Different frequency levels allow more than one level of creation to exist in the same spatial area without interfering with each other. Each realm has its own seventh-level race. See Five New Realms of Light.

Sequential Light Codes. A series of light transmissions which, by nature, require that the entire sequence be transmitted before the results are manifested. See New Codes of Sequential Phasing.

Simultaneous Time. The concept that past, present and future are all blended into a single, ongoing reality.

Sleep of the Ages. The healing process experienced by an individual who has recently crossed over from physical to etheric realms. Often this takes place within the Valley of the Final Sleep.

Solar Center of the Human Heart. A physical location in the human heart where light pulses from the Sun trigger energy releases throughout the body. This energy is utilized by the blood in healing and revitalizing the body. Solar essence previously expressed through the human mind will soon be expressed and refined through this heart solar center.

Solar Initiation. Solar radiance will intensify within the Solar Center of the Human Heart until it overflows into Earth's atmosphere, transmuting all discord into total harmony and love.

Temple of the Octave. An etheric "structure" utilized in the healing processes following death. Each of the Temple's eight separate phases relates to a separate level of awareness in the individual consciousness.

Universal Coordinate Pattern. The grid design or pattern within the universal grid system of the galaxy that establishes the placement of stars and other heavenly bodies. Similar to a stellar map.

Universal Energy. The basic form of pure raw energy — free from any informational content. It may be utilized to upgrade a planet's vibratory rate, as is presently being done on Earth.

Valley of the Final Sleep. One of several names given to the etheric region where many souls go immediately after crossing over from the physical worlds. See Sleep of the Ages.

Veil of Forgetfulness. A veil of energy placed around the Earth at the request of the human race when it chose this planet. Based on its own internal needs, the race wished to develop in apparent isolation. This veil inhibits individuals from recognizing their divine nature and from remembering the ongoing nature of life through cycles of birth and death. It also restricts our recognition of the intelligence and vitality of all parts of the universe.

Illumination arts is pleased to make available one of the most beautiful books of all time:

Shortly before his passing, Kahlil Gibran wrote:

"I go, but if I go with a truth not yet voiced, that very truth will again seek me and gather me, though my elements be scattered throughout the silences of eternity, and again shall I come before you that I may speak with a voice born anew out of the heart of those boundless silences."

Now, more than 40 years later, Jason Leen has brought forth **The Death of the Prophet**—the powerful, beautiful completion of Gibran's immortal trilogy. **The Prophet**, the first book of this trilogy, is one of the most widely-read books in history and is considered a literary masterpiece.

🌿 🌿 🌿

"Anybody who loved Kahlil Gibran's book The Prophet and/or The Garden of the Prophet will like this new addition. It is truly Gibran's masterful writing, and I love it!" —**Elisabeth Kubler-Ross**

"A work of art...awe inspiring in its grace....The mystical beauty is apparent throughout....a true completion of Gibran's trilogy."
—**Scott Miners**
The Turning Point Bulletin

"For me, this is Gibran's greatest work. It has become my constant companion, my friend. Here, I am reminded and inspired by the wonder of life and the magnificence of my own existence." —**Terry McBride,** author
Getting Well, Staying Well,
and *Everybody Wins*

Quality trade paperback, 96 pages, perfect bound, with cover art by William Brooks. Available from your local bookstore or from:

ILLUMINATION ARTS
177 Telegraph Road, Suite 361, Bellingham, WA 98226

For each copy, enclose $7.95 U.S. plus $2.00 for shipping and handling.